Feast Your Eyes On This

Food & YOU Devotional Cookbook
by
Tianna Feaster

Photography by Antar Hanif
Food Styling by Lisa Cherkasky

credits

Feast Your Eyes on This, Food & You Devotional Cookbook
Copyrights © 2011 by Tianna Feaster
Independently published by Tianna Feaster
District Heights, Maryland 20747
www.cheftianna.com

Printed in: USA

Edited by Patricia Marshall
Cover and Layout Design by Ralston Cyrus & Brian D. Johnson of Doran Designs, LLC
Nutritional Facts by Juvonia Harris RD, LDN
Photography, Antar Hanif
Makeup Artist, Nichelle Lewis
Food Stylist, Lisa Cherkasky

ISBN: 978-0-615-75657-8

Definition References
Brainy-Quote.com
Merriam-Webster.com

Disclaimer:
Sodium occurs naturally in many foods. Our diets will never be sodium free because we actually need sodium to help maintain the right balance of fluids in our bodies. Sodium also helps transmit nerve impulses and to influence the contraction and relaxation of muscles. Do not attempt to deprive the body of this mineral. We are going to eat sodium. It is however important to try to keep this amount to the recommended daily intake of less than 2300 mg/day. If you eat a high sodium food, learn to compliment that food with a very low sodium food such as a fresh vegetable, fruit or other non-processed food item.

All rights reserved. No part of this publication may be reproduced, stored in retrieval system, or transmitted in any form or by any means-electronic, mechanical, digital, photocopy, recording or any other without prior permission of the author and publisher.

acknowledgements

Thank you, God for giving me the vision and providing the provisions to birth this book.

Mom, thank you for seeing the greatness in me when I could not see it in myself.

Teddy, the man who has a world for my ocean.

Juvonia, thanks for encouraging me to do the book.

Valerie, thank you for always being my cheerleader and believing in me and my vision; I finally got a product...lol

Bridget Bartlet, thank you for setting up the platform for me to blog for Essence; because of that I am able to do this cookbook.

J, thank you for helping me get through the photo shoot while I was recovering from surgery.

Tamika, thank you for your support and the use of your home for the photo shoot.

Special thanks to all my family and friends who have supported me along my journey and with this endeavor.

dedication

In loving memory of Phillip Allen Feaster ("Daddy")

Thank you for showering me with your unconditional love. I was so honored to be your daughter.

table of contents

forward ix *introduction* x

Part I – discovery 1

are you disciplined? 3 **early bird smoothie** 5
do your research 7 **broiled chicken salad w/tarragon & cranberries** 8
 roasted asparagus 9
it's a process 10 **fish tacos w/spicy chipotle remoulade** 13
not tomorrow but today 16 **sautéed rainbow swiss chard** 19
you cannot out exercise bad eating habits 20 **turkey bacon & veggie frittata** 23
consistency 24 **turkey chili** 26
 seared scallops w/pepper & tarragon sauce 27

Part II – the aha moments 29

are you enjoying the moment? 30 **grilled tuscan skirt steak** 33
are you accountable? 34 **lemon thyme herbed chicken marinade** 36
 phillip's turnips 37
when enough is enough! 38 **low fat mac & cheese w/ shrimp** 40
 sautéed kale 41
what does your margin look like? 42 **egg scrambler** 44
 pecan crusted chicken 45
are you comfortable with being comfortable? 46 **butternut squash orzo w/sage** 49
strength in the struggle 50 **whole wheat linguine w/shrimp, heirloom tomatoes, & basil** 53

Part III – fresh start — 55

dig deep inside of you	56
forgiveness	60
if there is a will, there is a way	64
starting over	69
letting go is a process	72
renewing your mind	76

roasted brussel sprouts	58
twice baked sweet potatoes	59
roasted sweet & white potatoes w/shallots & sage	63
the real deal phil burger	67
breakfast wrap	70
watermelon w/arugula & mint vinaigrette	71
brunch quiche	75
lemon herbed tilapia	79

Part IV – keeping it moving — 81

loving yourself the healthy way	82
what are we feeding our children	86
having an attitude of gratitude	90
knowing what to do and doing it	94
the 4c's to a healthy lifestyle	98
pay now or pay later	102
cool things to know about food & you	106

chicken stew	85
crunchy cornflake chicken tenders	88
apple salsa & brie puff pastry	89
sautéed green beans	92
make your own ("myo") grilled pizza	93
roasted orange balsamic cornish hens	97
grilled romaine lettuce w/ciabatta bread	101
harvest salad w/turkey tenderloins	104
champagne mango & basil salsa	105

foreword
by Andrea Roane, News Anchor, WUSA 9, Washington, D.C.

One in four Americans is obese and by the year 2014, nearly half of us will wear that label. And what an expensive label it is. According to the American Cancer Society, obesity costs our nation 147-billion dollars in direct medical costs each year.

Being obese or overweight increases the risk for developing several illnesses and various types of cancer, including breast cancer. Because breast cancer is the most common form of cancer among African-American women, and because the breast cancer mortality rate in the District of Columbia is the highest in the nation, in 1993, I initiated Buddy Check 9 on WUSA-TV. The goal of Buddy Check is to encourage women to take charge of their own breast health.

Every 9th of the month, I remind women to practice early detection, to do a monthly breast self exam, schedule their annual mammogram and regular clinical exam and to get their Buddy to do the same. A Buddy can be a spouse, a relative, friend or co-worker.

Besides early detection, weight control, physical activity and dietary choices are the most effective methods for reducing the country's obesity epidemic and, in turn, lowering the risk for breast cancer.

That means what we eat and how we prepare our food is critical to overall nutrition and health. But knowing what to do is not always easy to do. Sometimes we need a "Buddy" to help us make those better choices.

Personal Chef Tianna Feaster is that "Buddy".

Getting us to eat healthy and well is what this "Buddy" is all about. Tianna believes "food should not only enliven your taste buds and fill your stomach, but should also provide nutritional value and be beneficial to your health and lifestyle."

Her food philosophy fits right in line with First Lady Michelle Obama's campaign to get Americans moving and eating right.

Tianna was an immediate hit with viewers on WUSA-TV. She is a regular food contributor inspiring viewers to get fit, eat healthy and to change their lifestyles permanently. Her recipes are delicious, nourishing, and a feast for the eyes!
I am honored to introduce you to Tianna Feaster, first-time author and personal chef on the move.

introduction

Food, food, food... Sometimes food consumes our thoughts. "What will I eat? Where will I eat?" "What's for breakfast, lunch or dinner? What can I snack on? Where should I order carryout?" Food is a main focus especially if you have a family to feed and a hectic work schedule. Let's not forget those who are on a tight budget, with limited time to cook, it's easier to just stop at a fast food establishment and get a value meal or order from the dollar menu. These choices usually answer the question of "What's for dinner?"

The questions we really should be asking are, "What am I feeding my children? Is this good for our health? How will this affect our blood pressure, glucose level, or heart?" We don't always ask those questions until we are in a doctor's office's or hospital receiving an unexpected diagnosis of our rapidly deteriorating health.

I grew up living the ideal healthy lifestyle. We ate well, and I was very athletic. Although deep down, I wanted to experience the taste of what I thought would be a good burger from one of those carryouts we use to regularly pass. I recall asking for a burger from one place in particular, and my dad responded, "I will go home and make you a real burger." Of course I was confused and heart broken by his response because I thought everyone had "real burgers." The older I got, the more I understood and appreciated the choices he made for me.

I remember going to farms in the Washington metropolitan area, picking fresh fruits and vegetables. Our meats came from the butcher shop. Canned food was foreign to me. My dad diligently exercised and ate very well. He promoted a healthy lifestyle by example. Eventually, he strayed from that lifestyle when we were older. He worked so much that he didn't have time to exercise like he was use to doing. He also developed some poor eating habits along the way. He would sit up late at night and eat salty chips, cookies, ice cream and pies. It got so bad; my mother had to hide his goodies from him. Don't get me wrong, he still ate fresh fruits and veggies. As a result of eating poorly and not exercising, he gained weight. Later he was diagnosed with Congestive Heart Failure (CHF). Did his actions contribute to his CHF? Or, could it have been his lack of exercise? Yes, all of these choices were contributions to congestive heart failure. Prior to learning about his illness, my dad attempted some diets but they were unsuccessful due to lack of commitment.

When I left home to live on campus, I strayed from healthy eating too. I didn't have much of a choice since I was away from home cooked meals. Mostly I would eat cafeteria food, which wasn't healthy at all but it satisfied the hunger. Other times, I would go to fast food places to eat pizza, burgers and/or fries. As a result of my upbringing, I am a food snob; therefore, I have always been wise about where and what I consumed. I believe if you are going eat fast food, then it should be from a high quality establishment. I maintained my routine exercise, but it didn't matter since I was still eating what was available to me on a daily basis. Many of the foods I consumed consisted of hormones; therefore, I could not out exercise my poor eating habits. Eating poorly made me feel sluggish. There is nothing worse than being tired when you are trying to be productive throughout the day.

Food can have both positive and negative effects on the body depending on the ingredients as well as our portion size. My dad's battle with CHF made me food and weight conscious. I became so attentive to my weight and other people's weight. Also, I became label conscious of all foods I purchased. I researched everything before allowing it to enter my body. Some people would think I went overboard, but what happened to me, I hope happens to others, in that I made a lifestyle change. I decided to respect and love my body. I believe as long as I treat my body right, my body will treat me right.

Making a choice to eat and live a healthy lifestyle was a huge responsibility. Not only did I have to consider the foods that I eat but also the portions. Eating a salad is a healthy choice, but it becomes unhealthy after adding too much dressing to it. For example, too much salad dressing can increase your calories and sodium intake. Therefore, monitoring my portions became essential to this lifestyle change.

I try to keep a fairly low carb diet, with no more than two "splurge" days per week. My typical daily meal consists of the following:
- Breakfast – Scrambled egg whites with diced tomatoes, and oatmeal with blueberries
- Lunch – Seared salmon with sautéed spinach, and an orange
- Dinner – Grilled chicken breast with a mixed green salad
- And my favorite part of the day is when I get my snack on with Flaxseed/Multigrain Tostitos with Black Bean Corn Salsa (Trader Joes).

My "splurge" days look like the following:
- Pizza (My favorite is from Matchbox DC.)
- Onion straws
- A slice of cheesecake (My favorite is from the Cheesecake Factory.)

We face many circumstances and challenges in our lives that may cause us to stray away from what is healthy for us. Don't give up. Get back on the right track. I encourage you to take this journey with me to live a healthy lifestyle.

discovery

are you disciplined?

discovery

One day while working out with my trainer at 5:30am, I thought, "It takes a lot of discipline to get up every morning to be consistent with a workout routine." In life, not only do we have to be consistent, but we have to stay disciplined. DISCIPLINE is what keeps us consistent. Discipline is a system of rules of conduct or methods of practice. It involves training to improve strength and self-control.

Let's take a look at our daily lives, especially with this crazy economy that has forced Americans to become disciplined in many areas. Due to all of the economic changes, we really had to cut back and become more disciplined with our spending habits. Instead of dining out, people have become more budget conscious. They eat out less and choose to bring their lunches to work. Honestly, not only are we saving money, but it gives us an opportunity to prepare healthier dishes, which forces us to be more disciplined with our appetites. Our leaner finances give us new opportunities to live smarter and healthier. Preparation of healthier dishes is a discipline that is one benefit towards leaner living. I know being disciplined can be hard but YOU can do it! Setting a few realistic goals, renewing your mind and being consistent will lead to discipline, not only with your eating and exercising but, also with your overall lifestyle.

When we aren't disciplined, things start to spiral out of control. When our lives (i.e. finances, family, work, and our physical, mental and spiritual health) begin to spiral out of control, it is because, somewhere, there is a lack of discipline.

So, remember to be disciplined. I know it's hard because it's so easy to return to old habits. The definition of discipline states that it helps to gain control. Let's all practice self-control when it comes to our eating and exercising habits. I know I will, and if I can do it, so can YOU!

discovery

early bird smoothie

ingredients:

1 cup Stonyfield fat free French Vanilla yogurt

1 cup strawberries, chopped

1 cup blueberries

2 bananas, sliced

2 tsp honey

1 handful of ice

directions:

Place the strawberries into a food processer and blend for one minute. This will prevent your smoothie from being so lumpy. Add your blueberries, bananas, honey and fat free yogurt and process for an additional minute for that smooth delicious taste. Wow, I can almost taste it! How about you? Now add your ice and process again for another minute. Pour into a 12oz glass and serve immediately. This is a great start to your first day of discipline.

Serves 2
Calories 155; Fat 1g; Saturated Fat .5g; Carbohydrates 38.5g; Protein 34g;; Sodium 37mg; Fiber 3.25g

chef tianna's tips:

Not only is this particular smoothie a great way to get your antioxidants for the day, it is also a great way for your skin to look healthy and beautiful. You can use a kiwi instead of blueberries. Kiwi contains as much potassium as a banana and is rich in Vitamin A and E.

It is fine if you choose to use Greek yogurt, or low-fat yogurt, however, my preference is the Stonyfield brand.

do your research!

discovery

Whenever you are getting ready to invest in anything in life (i.e. career, education, volunteerism, exercise routines, new diets, professional organizations, etc.) you have to do your research. You really need to know how to be involved and committed. When I shopped for a car, I recalled my friend Sima saying, "Feaster, you have to do your research." Well, she's right. It is important to have knowledge of whatever or wherever you are planning to get involved. Learn everything possible before you seize opportunities.

Some considerations need to be more deeply researched than others. You should not depend on people to inform you of all that you need to know, but it does help to learn about what others have experienced.

Other people's experiences could definitely assist so that you can determine how to meet your needs relative to standards, quality, and of course, the right price. It is important to formulate your own decisions. Therefore, gather information about:
- Relationships
- Facts
- Cost
- Pros
- Cons
- Qualifications
- Requirements

Similarly, when it comes to your spiritual, mental and physical health, DO YOUR RESEARCH! Resist acting on impulse and emotion. Make decisions after careful review and considerations. Oftentimes, we get on these crazy diets and try certain foods and we don't get the desired results because we didn't do our research and/or didn't count the cost of the investment. So we end up wasting money, food, and time. The end result – we are dissatisfied. Do your research and know where it leads. This also goes for recipes, exercise routines, diet choices, and even choosing a personal trainer. So, I encourage you to research whatever you choose to pursue. What might work well for others may not work for you.

discovery

broiled chicken salad w/ tarragon & dried cranberries

ingredients:

- ½ cup dried cranberries
- 2 tbsp fresh tarragon, chopped
- 2 celery stalks, finely chopped
- 2 tsp kosher salt
- 2 tsp black pepper
- Olive oil
- 1 lb skinless boneless chicken breasts, chopped into 1-2 inch cubes
- 1 cup mayonnaise (olive oil based)
- 2 tsp fresh lemon juice

directions:

Preheat the broiler to 425°F. Season the chicken breast with salt and pepper. Drizzle the broiler pan with olive oil and cook chicken for about 20 minutes or until done. "How can I be certain that my chicken is done after 20 minutes?" This is a good question. Take a fork and prick it. If it bleeds clear, then it is done. If it bleeds red, you have a problem. Cook until it is no longer red. After it is done, let the chicken rest, "cool", for about 2-5 minutes and chop chicken into 1-2 inch cubes.

In a large bowl, mix dried cranberries, celery, tarragon, mayonnaise and the chopped chicken. Refrigerate until ready to serve, preferably, 1 hour.

Serves 10
Calories 102; Fat 4g; Saturated Fat .8g; Carbohydrates 6g; Protein 15g; Sodium 210mg; Fiber .75g

chef tianna's tips:

*To cut down on cost, you can use thighs or **research** which would be more cost effective when you decide to make this delicious salad. By the way, thighs definitely have more flavor. During summer grilling, take some of your grilled chicken and chop it up and follow the directions for the chicken salad. This is best served over a bed of mixed greens, romaine lettuce or multi-grain/whole wheat bread. For a rotisserie chicken salad, just pull off the skin.*

discovery

roasted asparagus

ingredients:

1 lb fresh asparagus, trimmed

3 tbsp extra-virgin olive oil

½ tsp kosher salt

½ tsp cracked black pepper

2 garlic cloves, minced

directions:

Preheat oven to 425ºF. Spread asparagus in a single layer on a baking sheet and brush with olive oil. Sprinkle with salt, pepper and garlic. Roast a asparagus until the spears are tender when pricked with the tip of the knife; about 5-8 minutes depending on their thickness. Remove baking sheet from oven. Serve on platter and enjoy.

Serves 4
Calories 89; Fat 7g; Carbohydrates 4.5g; Protein 2.5g; Fiber 2.5g

chef tianna's tips:

Asparagus is a simple and quick vegetable to prepare. Many of my friends and family requested information on how to prepare asparagus without it becoming soggy. It's simple. My recommendation is after putting the asparagus on the baking sheet, place it under the broiler for 5-8 minutes or roast at 425°F for 5-8 minutes as instructed above. Asparagus is the cheapest and easiest side dish to prepare. Asparagus is great with steak, chicken, omelets or even in pasta. Spring is the best season to purchase asparagus. It is definitely the peak season for them.

it's a process

discovery

My friend Karima often sighs and says, "Everything is a process." I never knew why she would always say that, but now I know. There is a process for every aspect of life. What is a process? Is it a verb or a noun? Is it an action, or is it a thing? I believe that process is an action. When we engage in any process, we are developing our character. There is a process for getting in shape, learning how to eat properly, grieving a loss, and investing in your spiritual life. There is a process for pursuing your dreams, a new career, or even an education. I have learned through my own experiences that EVERYTHING is a process. There is no getting around it! Process cannot be avoided. You have to go through it and be patient with yourself and your circumstances. It's not easy. Trust and know that I am going through a process. Although I lost my father two years ago, my healing process is still in motion. Talk about a long process! I have gone through many phases of the healing process; the frustration and anger phases were the most challenging.

If you are trying to start eating right or incorporating better eating habits into your diet, remember, take it step-by-step. You cannot reasonably do it cold turkey. If you never drink water, start drinking 8-16 oz. a day and then increase it as you progress. If you drink sodas all day, reduce your soda intake to one a day or half a soda per day. If you eat at fast-food restaurants all the time, begin making your meals more often.

Another option is to look for low calorie or heart-healthy menu selections when you do eat out, so you can make better CHOICES! Look online and try new recipes (I have many recipes on my website.) When it comes to exercising, some of my friends say they cannot run; therefore, I encourage them to commit to walking short distances consistently then to gradually increase their distance levels. Now I encourage you to start off by walking down the street and then around the corner and before you know it, without even realizing it, 30 minutes have gone by, and you have covered your neighborhood.

Here are some tips to help you through your processes:
    1. Decide in your mind, "I want to make a change." (*Renew your mind.*)
    2. Begin reading up on things to help you stay encouraged. (*Do your research.*)
    3. Talk to a friend/family member/coworker about your experiences.
    4. Have an accountability partner.
    5. Take action. Start off small (eating, exercising, etc.).
    6. Stay consistent and be patient with yourself. If you have a relapse, re-group and press on. (Set small objectives to obtain your realistic goals.)

Remember you CAN do it, just start slow and know that each step is a process.

discovery

fish tacos w/
spicy chipotle remoulade

discovery

fish tacos w/ spicy chipotle remoulade

ingredients:

Fish (Pan Fry)

1 lb tilapia fillets, cut into slices/chunks

2 eggs, lightly beaten

Kosher salt & cracked black pepper

½ tsp garlic powder

1/3 cup all-purpose flour

2 cups Panko (Asian breadcrumbs)

1 cup canola oil

8 soft tortillas

Serves 4 (8 tacos)
Calories 114; Fat 3g; Saturated Fat .8g; Carbohydrates 8g; Protein 14g; Sodium 188mg; Fiber .3g

Slaw

1 cup cabbage, shredded

1 cup jicama, julienned

1 red bell pepper, julienned

2 tbsp rice wine vinegar

Kosher salt & black pepper

½ cup fresh lime juice

2 tsp chili powder

1 tbsp honey

¼ cup fresh cilantro, chopped

2 tbsp fat free, sour cream

Calories 30; Fat .25g; Saturated Fat 0g; Carbohydrates 7.2g; Protein .6g; Sodium 91mg; Fiber 1.7g

Pico de gallo

3 plum tomatoes, finely diced

¼ cup red onion, small diced

1 jalapeno, minced

¼ cup fresh cilantro, chopped

Juice of 2 fresh limes

2 cloves garlic, minced

Salt & pepper

Calories 21; Fat .25g; Saturated Fat 0g; Carbohydrates: 6g; Protein .5g; Sodium 84mg; Fiber .75g

Spicy Chipotle Remoulade

½ cup mayonnaise (olive oil based)

1 tbsp honey

2 tbsp fresh lime or lemon juice

1 tbsp capers

2 cloves garlic

1 Chipotle pepper

Salt & pepper

1 tbsp apple cider vinegar

Calories 78; Fat 6.7g; Saturated Fat 1g; Carbohydrates 5g; Protein: .13g; Sodium 159mg; Fiber .12g

discovery

directions:

Place the tilapia slices/chunks in a flat dish and season with salt, pepper and garlic powder. Then cover and refrigerate.

To make the remoulade, mix the mayonnaise, honey, lime or lemon juice, vinegar, chipotle pepper, capers, garlic and seasoning in a food processor and pulse until smooth. Cover and refrigerate.

To bread the fish, place the flour, eggs, and panko crumbs in three separate shallow dishes. Dip the fish pieces in flour, coating evenly, and shaking off any excess. Now dip fish in the eggs, and lastly into the panko crumbs, patting the pieces to help breadcrumbs hold. Set fish aside on a plate.

To cook the breaded fish, pour 1 cup of canola oil into a skillet to ¼ inch deep. Heat the oil at medium high heat. Cook the fish, turning until all sides are golden brown, and flesh is easily flaked with a fork. Drain on paper towels.

For the slaw, mix cabbage, red bell pepper, jicama, rice wine vinegar, seasoning, sour cream, honey, and lime juice in a bowl. Toss to coat evenly with the dressing.

For the pico de gallo, mix tomatoes, onion, cilantro, jalapeno pepper, lime juice, garlic, salt, and pepper together in a bowl. Refrigerate before serving.

chef tianna's tips:

You can use cod, mahi mahi or halibut in place of the tilapia. The fish is also great if you cook it in the oven, grilled and/or broiled.

As a treat for your children, this is a great way to make fish sticks and freeze later for another dinner or even lunch.

For children with gluten issues, use gluten free panko or rice chex cereal.

not tomorrow, but today!

discovery

In life, we often say, "Tomorrow, I'm going to start eating right. Tomorrow, I'm going to try to walk a mile a day. Tomorrow, I'm going to start telling someone I love them or start loving myself. One day, I'm going to take that trip, go back to school, and pursue my dreams. Tomorrow, I'm going to stop smoking. I'm going to start taking better care of myself." Why not today? Time is so precious and valuable. I lost my father, Phillip Feaster, to heart disease. He was an awesome man who had purpose. He was loving and giving. He just lived! My father took time to appreciate life and he didn't wait until tomorrow. He lived "in the moment!" That's what I loved about my Daddy!

My father had Congestive Heart Failure, which rendered his heart very weak. That increased the oxygen demand of the body tissue beyond the capability of the heart to deliver. He was also borderline diabetic. He did not wait to start improving his lifestyle. He found other ways to enjoy the simple pleasures in life. He started making better food choices by eating sugar free cookies and pies, incorporating lean meats, fruits and vegetables into his diet, and throughout the day, a certain amount of carbohydrates. Now, don't get me wrong, my father loved to eat and he ate great foods. He just had to continue to incorporate cardio exercise, which helps the heart significantly.

Remember, STOP putting your dreams, health, and self-improvement off until later. Don't wait, start today! After losing my father, who was very precious to me, I learned to live for today because tomorrow, we know, is not promised. Since the Health Care Reform bill has passed, everyone in America is afforded the opportunity to have better health care and to be accountable to ourselves.

discovery

sautéed rainbow swiss chard

ingredients:

1 large bunch fresh Swiss chard (Rainbow)

1 shallot, sliced

2 tbsp sunflower oil

Kosher salt & cracked black pepper

directions:

Rinse the Swiss chard thoroughly. Remove the stalk. Roughly chop the leaves into inch - wide strips. (If you are wondering how to chop it, do it like your mother and grandmother use to with their greens). Heat saucepan on a medium-high heat setting, add sunflower oil, (this will give it a buttery taste) and a few slices of shallots. Add the chopped Swiss chard. Add salt and pepper if needed. Cover for about 2-5 minutes. Flip the leaves over in the pan, making sure that the bottom is on the top. Check for chard to be tender and wilted. Add salt and pepper again if needed. Remove the Swiss chard. Eat and enjoy today.

Serves 4
Calories 88; Fat 7g; Saturated Fat .75g; Carbohydrates 6g; Protein 2.5; Sodium 245mg; Fiber 3g

chef tianna's tips:

For more favor (because they say fat is flavor) add some chopped bacon on top. If you desire to have pork bacon, use the center cut, which is the leanest cut . This Sautéed Rainbow Swiss Chard taste great with tilapia or chicken. Most people do not know that Swiss chard is a vegetable that they usually pass up in the grocery store.

you cannot out-exercise
bad eating habits!

discovery

I was at my community fitness center working out and taking classes called the Cardio Sweat Shop and the Flex and Pump. As I worked out, I saw all of these women working hard at their fitness routines. Surprisingly, when I looked around the room, I noticed something. They weren't really losing any weight. Why? Poor eating habits! That's why exercise cannot compensate for bad eating habits. You can go hard seven days a week and you won't lose your goal weight if you have poor eating habits. For example, when you make a salad and drown it in dressing, and cheese, etc., that totally defeats the purpose. Or even saying, "Well, I'm exercising later. I'll work it off." Exercising is not a ticket for "I can eat whatever I want." Everything has to be balanced. Weight loss is 20% exercise - the other 80% is – EATING! This reminds me of what I heard a trainer say, "You cannot out exercise bad eating habits." The first rule of thumb is eating in moderation. Your body craves and needs nutrients. Therefore, make sure you get all of your fruits, vegetables, protein, and complex carbohydrates daily. Don't forget to drink adequate amounts of water daily. Water is so important! Your water intake should be half your weight. That means if you're 134 lbs., you should be drinking 67 oz. of water daily. There is no better liquid to consume than healthy H_2O.

discovery

turkey bacon & veggie frittata

ingredients:

8 large egg whites or whole eggs

⅓ cup reduced fat sour cream

½ cup leeks, chopped

½ cup red bell pepper, julienned

½ cup orange bell pepper, julienned

½ cup asparagus, chopped

½ cup turkey bacon, chopped

½ cup reduced fat sharp shredded cheddar cheese

¼ tsp kosher salt

¼ tsp black pepper

directions:

In a large bowl, mix the eggs and sour cream together. Add veggies, bacon and cheese, and continue mixing. Add salt and pepper. Take a 10 inch ovenproof nonstick skillet and coat with cooking spray. Pour mixture into the pan and bake at 400°F for about 30-40 minutes. If it is a little loose in the middle put it under the broiler for 3-4 minutes. Serve immediately. While eating and enjoying this great dish, remember that you can't out exercise poor eating habits. Stay healthy.

Serves 6 - 8

Calories 97; Fat 4g; Saturated Fat 1.8g; Carbohydrates 5g; Protein 10g; Sodium 473mg; Fiber 1g

chef tianna's tips:

The kinds of veggies are optional. Any vegetables that you have left over in your fridge that need to be used, throw them in! Also, any other meat or seafood can be used.

consistency

discovery

In life, we often wonder why and ask these series of questions:
- Why can't I stick to this diet?
- Why isn't my career going to the next level?
- Why aren't I seeing any changes or progression in my life?
- Why are my kids resistant to my guidance?

There is one core thing. There is NO consistency. In every aspect of our lives, we have to be CONSISTENT!!! I read somewhere that we are not consistent because we are distracted and lose track of what is important.

What does consistent mean to you? What are the consequences when you are not consistent? There are several definitions of consistency. One definition I particularly like is from Brainy Quote: Consistency – Firmness of constitution or character, substantiality, durability, persistency. Well, in life we must be consistent with everything we do because, eventually, we will see the results. As a business owner, I have to stay consistent because if I don't, I won't effectively see the fruits of my labor or what needs to be changed. Healthy business growth develops through consistency. This would create excellence, which should be our core focus. Certainly, consistency is essential to meet the varied solid business goals. It's challenging but the rewards are worth it!

I really noticed the need for consistency when I started working out again after a mini break. You stop for a while and it takes a period for you to get back on track. That's why, to get the desired results, you have to stay consistent. It cannot happen overnight, but, with determination, you will succeed. That also holds true with eating right. You have to stay consistent. Okay, yes you can treat yourself but, remember, moderation is the key. I know a couple of ladies who are currently using a diet program, and to get positive results, they are being consistent. However, after they complete the diet they have to stay steadfast with healthy eating and exercising habits. It's a package deal. This should be applied to other areas of our life as well. We need to remain devoted to healthy goals. Sometimes we get DISTRACTED and caught up. We then find ourselves in awkward or bad situations.

Children learn positive habits when consistency is in practice. We can be consistent also with negative habits. Remember, adhering to any aspect of your life involves consistency. If you're not consistent with the positive changes that you are striving to make in your life, you cannot get the desired results. So, remember to be patient with yourself on this journey called life and stay - CONSISTENT. Trust me, positive benefits will surface. These benefits include, spiritual, mental, and physical health. As you enter into this new lifestyle change, I encourage you to practice consistency.

discovery

turkey chili

ingredients:

- 1 lb ground turkey
- 3 tbsp olive oil
- 1 medium yellow onion, chopped
- 5 cloves garlic, minced
- 1 tsp kosher salt
- 1 tsp black pepper
- 2 tsp chili powder
- 1 tsp fresh oregano, chopped
- 1 tsp cumin
- 1 tbsp tomato paste
- 1 chipotle chile en adobo, coarsely chopped
- 1 tbsp Chipotle sauce
- 1 (12oz) beer (preferably Corona)
- 1 (14 oz) can whole peeled tomatoes, with their juice
- 1 (15 oz) can kidney beans, rinsed and drained
- 1 (15 oz) can black beans, rinsed and drained
- 1 (15 oz) canned corn, rinsed and drained

directions:

Cook ground turkey in skillet. Break it up by chopping it with a spatula or spoon. While the ground turkey is cooking, heat the oil in a large, heavy pot over medium-high heat. Add the onion, garlic, salt, black pepper, cumin, chili powder, and oregano for about 3 minutes or until fragrant. Stir in the tomato paste and the chipotle chile and sauce, cook 1 minute more. Add cooked turkey to the sauce. Next, add beer and simmer until reduced by half, for 8 minutes. Add whole, peeled tomatoes, crushing them with your fingers. Put into the pot, along with their juices, the beans, and corn. Cook uncovered, stirring occasionally, until thick for about 10-20 minutes. While waiting, take the time to read Consistency (page 25). Ladle the chili into bowls. Eat and enjoy!

Serves 8-10
Calories 583; Fat 14.8g; Saturated Fat 2.6g; Carbohydrates 28.6g; Protein 18.6g; Sodium 583mg; Fiber 5.3g

chef tianna's tips:

To give your chili a little touch of flavor, add chopped scallions, cilantro, a slice of avocado (rich in vitamin A), fat free sour cream or smoked Gouda/Monterey Jack cheese. This dish is also great with a tossed or mixed greens salad. To cut down on your sodium intake, you can buy unsalted tomatoes.

If you have any left over chili, freeze it for your next chili night. Freezing suggestions: Take one cup and put it in a Ziploc bag. Do not forget to seal out the air.

discovery

seared scallops w/ yellow pepper & tarragon sauce

ingredients:

1lb large "dry" sea scallops

2 tbsp extra-virgin olive oil

Kosher salt & freshly ground pepper

For the Sauce:

2tbs. extra-virgin olive oil

1 tbsp minced garlic (2 large cloves)

1 fresh Serrano chile or Jalapeno, minced

½ yellow bell pepper, finely diced (1/3 cup)

1 tbsp fresh lime juice

2 tbsp of fresh tarragon, coarsely chopped

Kosher salt & freshly ground black pepper

directions:

Cooking the scallops:
Rinse the scallops and pat dry with a paper towel. Season with salt and pepper. Heat a 10-12 inch nonstick skillet over medium-high heat for 1-2 minutes. Heat the oil until quite hot. Place scallops in pan and sear. To ensure consistency, check each side to make sure scallops are brown, crisp and firm to the touch. Take pan off the heat and transfer scallops to a plate, and set in a warm spot. Let pan rest for a minute before you make the sauce.

Making the sauce:
Return the pan to medium heat. Add oil, garlic and chile; then sauté until fragrant for about 30 seconds. Add bell peppers and sauté until the pepper is barely soft, about 1 minute. Add the lime juice and simmer to reduce slightly for 30 to 60 seconds. Stir in the tarragon. Reduce the heat to low and return scallops and any excess juices to the pan. Gently roll the scallops around to coat them in the sauce. Add salt and pepper if needed.

Serves 2-3

Calories 257; Fat 14g; Saturated Fat 2g; Carbohydrates 7g; Protein 25g; Sodium 645mg; Fiber .6g

chef tianna's tips:

After touching the jalapeno, do not touch your skin. If you do, you will burn all day, lol!

the aha moment

are you enjoying
the moment?

the aha moment

In this technology age, we are constantly on the go. We want things instantaneously! We are constantly driven at hectic paces, and prone to be accessible all of the time via various forms of communication on phones (texting, talking, listening, photographing, gaming), and frequent engagement on the Internet, including e-mail transmissions. This causes us to have less patience, to make unwise time investments, and to have less balance to appreciate our lives with loved ones. We are constantly pressed to get to the next level. Clearly, we are more mobile and accessible but increasingly out of touch with what is most meaningful for contentment in life.

During our times of ripping and running, we find ourselves and family members constantly eating junk foods, not getting enough rest, and you know we're not exercising because by the time we sit down, we are what?–TIRED!! Frequently, we're challenged with how to balance home, work, and leisure. The daily grinds of life and our hectic paces have left us largely unable to have contentment and satisfaction from the precious moments that life has to offer. We need to properly weigh our priorities and be sure to regularly include quality time with our family and friends.

Before you know it, you look around and think, "I'm not appreciating the moments in my life." Even I'm guilty of it. I'm so guilty of frenzied habits and striving to reach the next level versus the placement of balance in my life. My dad would say, "T, slow down and enjoy your moments. Don't rush." I have realized so much about life since my father has passed. My dad definitely enjoyed his moments. When he was home, he was at home and when he was at work, he was at work. I finally decided *enough is enough*; I needed to appreciate all of the moments. Think BALANCE because balance has proven to contribute to the gains of pleasure in life.

It helps to remember that life is not a rehearsal. We often tend to multitask versus getting better at time management and establishing priorities. Lack of balance in our lives can lead to frustration, anxiety, and stress related illnesses. It's just not healthy. Put preventative measures in place. Slow down and savor your moments with yourself, your family and friends. Take that walk, run, swim, do other forms of exercise, and join a fitness program. Don't deprive yourself of life at its fullest.

Make great healthy meals for yourself and for your family and friends. Indulge wisely. Life will reward your healthy choices. Recognize that it is not the amount of time you have, but what you choose to do with it. Go for the gusto! So, get out there and gain the best from your moments!

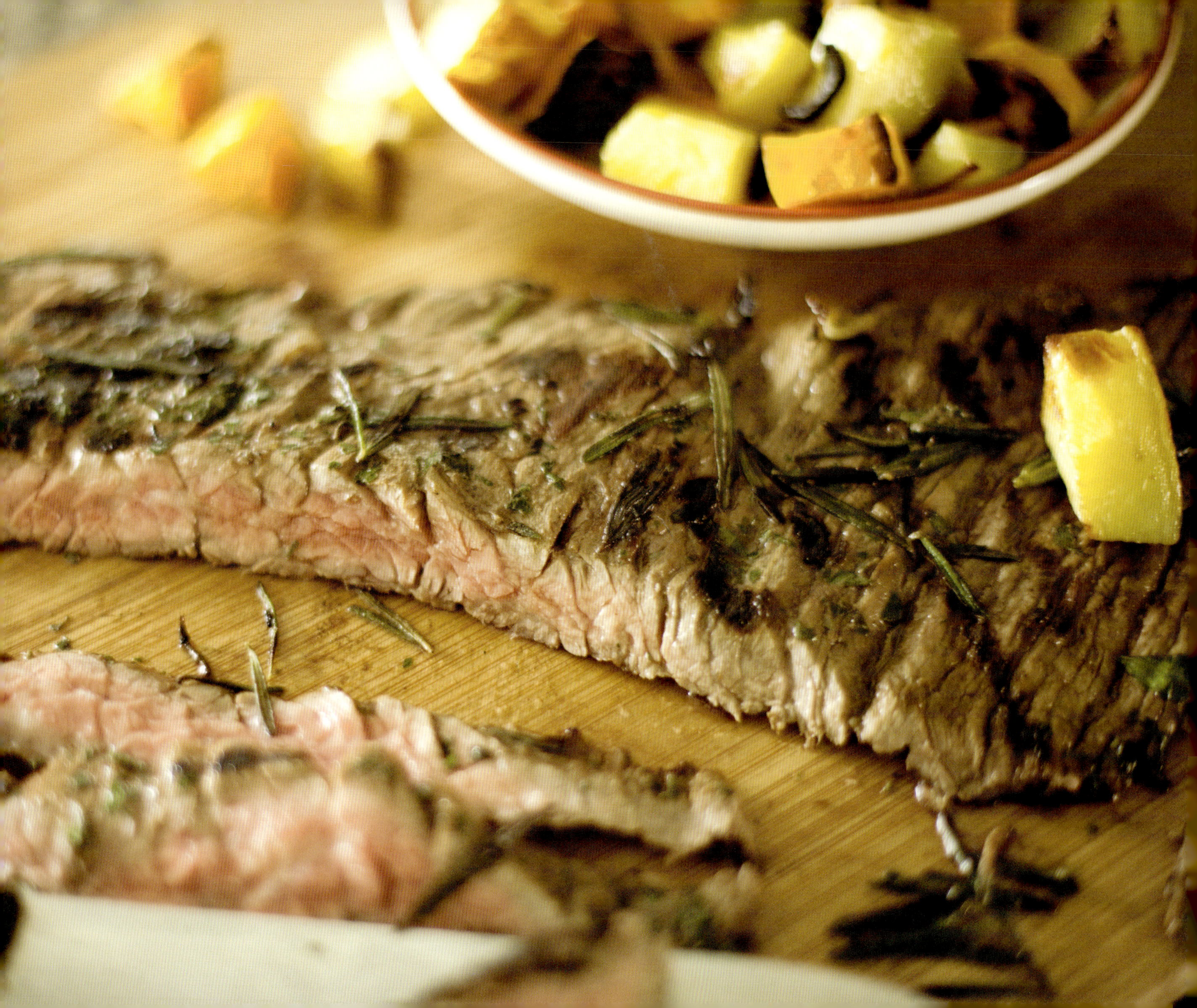

the aha moment

grilled tuscan skirt steak

ingredients:

1 ¼ to 1 ½ lb skirt steak, trimmed

Kosher salt

Freshly ground cracked pepper

½ cup extra-virgin olive oil or olive oil

3 tbsp apple cider vinegar

3 tbsp Worcestershire sauce

1 tbsp fresh rosemary leaves, chopped

3 cloves garlic, minced

1 tbsp fresh Italian (flat leaf) parsley, chopped

directions:

Prepare a medium-high grill (charcoal, gas or electric grill). While the grill is preheating, rub your steak with garlic, salt, pepper, parsley, rosemary and extra virgin olive oil. Add Worcestershire sauce and vinegar. Grill the steak, turning occasionally (5-8 minutes) until prepared to medium-well. Move the steak to a cutting board and let rest for 3 minutes. The steak needs to rest because it is still cooking. Cut each piece crosswise into 4–6 inch-long pieces and then, holding your knife at a slight angle, cut each piece on a bias (across the grain into the slices). Enjoy the moment while you are eating this delicious Grilled Tuscan Skirt Steak.

Serves 4

Calories 524; Fat 42.2; Saturated Fat 9.75g; Carbohydrates 1.25g; Protein 33.5g; Sodium 411mg; Fiber .25g

chef tianna's tips:

For all of my "well-done" lovers out there, please do not overcook the steak. For best results, the steak must be medium to medium-well in order for you to get its true flavor. If you don't have a grill, you can use the broiler that is located in your oven. Remember some broilers can be located in the oven or on the bottom. For the broiler, set temperature to 450ºF or medium-high heat.

Allowing your steak to marinate for 24 hours definitely brings out the flavors. This Grilled Tuscan Skirt Steak is best served with roasted or baked potato and roasted asparagus.

are you accountable?

the aha moment

My friend, Sima, and I were having a conversation one morning about how many people these days view it as a treat to be able to sit down at tables with their families to eat and appreciate well balanced meals. Have we really succumbed to this? We cannot depend on the health care system to take care of us. We have a responsibility to do our parts in the areas of prevention and healthy habits. Are we taking care of ourselves or being examples for our families? We cannot blame our poor food choices on the eating establishments. We have free will. Life is about choices. If you choose to frequently go to a fried chicken establishment, that is your choice. Regular consumption of such food is certainly a poor diet choice. Now, don't get me wrong, there is nothing wrong with fried chicken every once in awhile, but it shouldn't be routinely eaten. There are much healthier options.

One morning, I was watching Sunday's Best on CBS and they were discussing obesity and how it is a huge and costly epidemic. That's one important reason why we need to evaluate our food choices to select what is healthy for us and our families. I know we all have busy schedules but we should balance our lives to allow time to benefit our overall well-being – mind, soul and body. In our family planning decisions, the one thing we often ask is, "What are we going to eat tonight?" Frequently, we think of foods that are quick and fast. Somehow the focus is not healthy, well balanced meals, especially for folks who are constantly on the go. Regularly eating out causes you to select unhealthy choices; the results being health issues due to all the hormones, steroids, antibiotics, sodium, and fats in fast food selections.

The same amount of money you spend going out to eat can be used at the grocery store, shopping seasonally, and preparing FANTABULOUS meals for you and your family. Those actions represent accountability, wisdom, and responsibility. An added bonus is that you're investing in, and enriching treasured relationships. Eating together can present opportunities to decompress, collect thoughts, communicate with your family, and find out what is going on in your household.

So before you eat your next meal, remember Chef 'Tianna's 4 P's" of preparing a healthy meal:
- Plan your meals- (Prepare a schedule of your daily food menu.)
- Purchase seasonal items and save money. Learn what foods are in season.
- Prep – Prior to cooking, marinate and season your meats. My friend, Shannon, who has four kids, preps lasagna, turkey meat loaf, and even mashed potatoes. She then freezes them. When she is ready to cook what she has prepared, she just pops the dishes in the oven. (Note: If you do your prepping early, you can do other things while your dinner is cooking.)
- Prepare meals that are quick and healthy or choose a day to prepare several meals for the week.

the aha moment

lemon thyme herbed chicken marinade

ingredients:

4- 4 oz chicken cutlets

3 tbsp fresh thyme, chopped

2 cloves garlic, minced

1 tbsp fresh lemon juice

1 tsp lemon zest

½ tsp kosher salt & fresh black pepper

⅓ cup extra-virgin olive oil

directions:

To make the marinade, first prep the thyme by removing it from the sprigs and then combine olive oil, thyme, minced garlic, lemon juice and one teaspoon of lemon zest. Also add salt and fresh black pepper. Now, whisk all of the ingredients together. Next, pour the marinade over the chicken cutlets in an airtight container with lid or place in a Ziploc bag to allow the chicken to marinate for about an hour.

Serves 4
Calories 287; Fat 14g; Saturated Fat 2g; Carbohydrates 3g; Protein 35g; Sodium 110mg; Fiber 2g

chef tianna's tips:

For the best flavor, marinate the chicken overnight. This quick and easy marinade will spruce up that chicken breast, thighs or wings just lying around in your freezer. Enjoy this delicious dish any night of the week.

the aha moment

phillip's (daddy) turnips

ingredients:

3 medium sized turnips

Kosher salt

Black pepper

2 tbsp of natural sugar (do not use artificial sweeteners)

3 tbsp of olive oil or extra virgin olive oil

1 tbsp of unsalted butter

2 strips of bacon (optional)

directions:

Peel and chop your turnips into ½ inch cubes or pieces. Make sure that the turnips are the same size so that they cook evenly.

Set your oven to 425ºF – 450ºF high broil. Place bacon on cooking sheet with foil (to make it easy to clean up). Cook for about 8 minutes or until bacon is nice and crispy.

Heat the pan over medium to medium high heat. To your pan, add 3 tbsp of olive oil and 1 tbsp of butter. Once the butter is melted, add your turnips. Add a small amount of salt, black pepper, and sugar and cook until turnips are golden brown and tender. Cover and cook the turnips for about 10 minutes. Stir and continue cooking for an additional 20 minutes. This would be a good time to read Are You Accountable (page 34). Remove turnips from pan and place on plate. Take your bacon and crumble on top of turnips as a garnish and for flavor. Enjoy.

Serves 4-6

Calories 125; Fat 7.5g; Saturated Fat 3g; Carbohydrates 14g; Fiber 2g; Protein 1g; Sodium 123 mg

chef tianna's tips:

Sugar gets rid of the bitter taste of turnips. If you are a diabetic, use one tbsp of natural sugar (do not use artificial sweeteners). Remember when shopping for bacon, always get the center cut bacon; this is the best quality bacon. This dish is best served over collard or kale greens.

when enough is enough!

the aha moment

The holiday season is a time for family gatherings and sharing with others. It is a time when we express how thankful we are, not only for the great food placed before us, but our gratitude for our family and friends, as well. During the holiday season, we tend to pile up our plates. Recently, I read an article on portion control. Portions are very important when it comes to preparing and consuming food. As a personal chef, one of THE important things I discuss with my clients is the understanding and mindset of portion control. Portion control allows you to watch how much you are eating throughout the day. Eating healthy small portions helps keep your metabolism in proper order.

When I was at my family reunion a couple of years ago, there was an open buffet for breakfast at the hotel. Folks were just piling up their plates with bacon, sausage, potatoes, pancakes, waffles, and scrambled eggs. It was out of control! I could feel my arteries clogging as I watched people eat the food that was piled on their plates. I thought to myself, "Why are they doing that? It is extremely unhealthy and it makes you sluggish." I believe it is essential to have the right focus about eating properly. As my mom says, "Sometimes your eyes are bigger than your stomach." That is so true.

People would feel better and be healthier if they knew how to select nutritious foods and to consume reasonable portions. I recommend visually dividing your food with proper amounts of protein, fresh fruits/vegetables and complex carbohydrates. Make sure that half of your plate has veggies/fruits and the other half has meat/fish, pasta, rice, etc. Keep it balanced.

I know you are saying, "Tianna, I want to enjoy the wonderful food and treats." Absolutely, I think you should, but too much of anything is not wise. Do everything in moderation. You don't have to pile your plate all at once. If you did not have enough, you can get more later. It's okay to push back from the table sometimes and tell yourself, "I've had enough."

the aha moment

low fat mac & cheese w/ shrimp

ingredients:

2 cups reduced fat cottage cheese

1 cup reduced fat sour cream

1 egg, beaten

1 tsp salt

1 tsp black pepper

2 cloves garlic, minced

2 cups reduced fat cheddar cheese

½ cup Gruyere cheese, shredded

1 lb peeled & deveined shrimp

1 8 oz elbow macaroni, drained (Whole wheat, optional)

¼ cup of Panko (Asian bread crumbs)

directions:

Preheat oven to 350º F. Remove shell from shrimp and season with salt and pepper. In a large mixing bowl, combine cottage cheese, sour cream, egg, salt, garlic, and black pepper. Add cheddar and gruyere cheeses and blend well. Add shrimp. Cook macaroni as directed on package and drain well. Add cooked macaroni to cheese mixture and blend until well coated. Add macaroni mixture to a greased 2 or 2 ½ quart baking dish and bake, uncovered, for 25-30 minutes.

Serves 10
Calories 254; Fat 2.3g; Saturated Fat 1.2g; Carbohydrates 11.9g; Protein 29.5g; Sodium 942.5mg; Fiber 1.5g

chef tianna's tips:

Panko breadcrumbs are optional. If you cannot find Gruyere cheese, use a low fat Swiss cheese instead. Shrimp are optional.

This is a great side dish to freeze. For portion control, put the Mac and cheese in muffin pans and freeze for later. A little of this goes a long way.

the aha moment

sautéed kale

ingredients:

1 large bunch of fresh kale

1 shallot slice

2-3 tbsp sunflower oil

1 -2 tbsp sherry vinegar, (apple cider vinegar is optional)

Kosher & cracked black pepper

directions:

Rinse the kale leaves thoroughly. Remove the stalk. Roughly chop the kale leaves into inch wide strips. Heat skillet on a medium heat, add sunflower oil and a few shallots. Add the chopped kale. Add salt and black pepper. Cover for about 2-5 minutes. Flip the kale leaves over in the pan, making sure that it cooks evenly on both sides. The kale should be tender and wilted. Add salt and pepper as needed. Remove the kale. Eat and enjoy; however, know when enough is enough!

Serves 4
Calories 91; Fat 7g; Saturated fat .75g; Carbohydrates 6g; Protein 2g; Sodium 25mg; Fiber 1g

chef tianna's tips:

To cut down on cooking time, you can buy pre-chopped kale.
Great with any main entree' or with Philip's Turnips (page 37).

what does your
margin look like?

the aha moment

I was in church one Sunday and my pastor spoke on the topic of margins, as in physical margins. The question is, "Do you have margins when it comes to eating and exercising?" Sometimes the things that we put in our bodies are simply not good for us and many times we don't exercise. Due to poor planning and preparation, we tend to eat when we get around to it, which leaves us subject to poor choices, and thoughts such as these seem to creep in, "I need something quick. I'm tired and hungry. I don't feel like cooking. I'll go to a fast food place and get something off the value menu."

I am back again to one of my core words, CHOICES! Keep the awareness that you need to have physical margins in your life. By now, you are probably thinking, "Tianna, what do you mean by margin?" Margin is that amount of space we allocate between our limits and loads before we hit that wall. If we don't have margin in our diets, we get to a point where we neglect ourselves so much that we end up paying for it later. You wonder why you're so tired or why you keep out growing your clothes, or why you're battling with borderline diabetes, heart disease, high cholesterol, or why you're mentally exhausted. There is NO margin. Necessary boundaries need to stay in place. Conquer your doubts and proceed to triumph!

We have to make sure we are constantly restoring our physical health by eating and exercising properly. Overall, our good health is not only a plus for us but for others, as well. Our purposes in life can be effective when we understand the need to have margin.

the aha moment

egg scrambler

ingredients:

8 eggs or egg whites, beaten

3 strips bacon or turkey bacon cooked and chopped

¾ cup fresh spinach, chopped

3 tomatoes, seeded and chopped

¾ cup red onion, chopped

¾ cup reduced fat shredded cheddar cheese or fat free feta

Kosher salt & black pepper

1 tbsp olive oil

directions:

Heat olive oil in a non-stick skillet on medium-high heat. Sautee onions, tomatoes, and wilt spinach in olive oil. Whisk eggs in a separate bowl. Add salt and pepper to taste. (Don't forget to watch that margin; you know, that amount of space between your limits and loads before going overboard.) Once the veggies are tender, add eggs. Scramble the eggs with the veggies. Then add the bacon. Add cheese and mix to melt. Eat and enjoy!

Serves 4

Calories 238; Fat 13g; Saturated Fat 5g; Carbohydrates 13g; Protein 18; Sodium 492mg; Fiber 2g

chef tianna's tips:

The kinds of veggies are optional. Any vegetables that you have left over in your fridge that need to be used, throw them in! Also, any other meat (ham, chicken, or sausage) or seafood (salmon, shrimp, or crab) can be added.

the aha moment

pecan crusted chicken

ingredients:

2 large eggs

8 chicken tenderloins

½ cup pecans, chopped

½ cup plain whole wheat bread crumbs

¼ tsp ground nutmeg

Kosher salt & pepper

¼ cup canola oil

directions:

Combine pecans, bread crumbs, half of the nutmeg, salt and pepper, to taste, in a food processor and grind. Pour onto a plate. Season chicken with salt, pepper and remaining half of the nutmeg. In a large bowl beat eggs. Dip the chicken in eggs and coat with pecan and bread crumb mixture and set aside on a baking sheet.

Heat oil in a large nonstick skillet over medium to medium-high heat. Add tenderloins and cook 5-8 minutes on each side. To determine if the chicken is done, prick with a fork. If the chicken bleeds clear, it's done. Of course if chicken bleeds red, continue cooking. After the chicken is done, transfer chicken to a plate. Eat and enjoy. Remember, maintain a healthy margin and do not over eat. This chicken is so good you will want more than the allowed portion.

Serves 4

Calories 292; Fat 18g; Saturated Fat 2.5g; Carbohydrates 12g; Protein 21g; Sodium 324mg; Fiber 2g

chef tianna's tips:

If you use a thick boneless chicken breast, split it into 5-6 tenderloins.
If you choose to bake the chicken, preheat the oven to 375 ºF for 20-25 minutes.
Pecan Crusted Chicken is great on mixed salad greens, asparagus, kale or brussels sprouts.
❄ You can freeze the pecan crusted chicken and save for family night. I recommend making chicken fingers for the children.

are you comfortable with being comfortable?

the aha moment

As I drive around town, transition comes to mind. There are season and weather changes. We have to make seasonal adjustments in our attire, diets, and in our exercise routines. Certain foods boost our immune system. Seasonal, as well as other adjustments, have an effect on our lifestyles. Change causes us to have to step out of our comfort zones, which causes us to be uncomfortable. Let's be open-minded and receptive to the process of positive change. Often, we fear change because it is in the unknown. Life is better, though, when we yield to necessary changes.

One day I asked my coworkers to sample a dish I'd prepared. They all declined because the ingredients were unfamiliar to them. They were uncomfortable with the unknown. I just laughed and said, "More for me." Although my coworkers said the dish smelled good, they couldn't overcome the unfamiliarity. Sometimes when we are in unknown territory, we prejudge and even complain about how the unfamiliar makes us feel. My personal trainer once told me that we have to find comfort even in uncomfortable situations. When I'm training, sometimes I yell out, "This is uncomfortable. This hurts." My trainer says, "Sometimes you have to be uncomfortable to get better results." That is so true. When it comes to preparing and trying various foods that are good for us, we need to conquer our reservations. I have learned that it's very easy, in life, to surrender to less than the best. However, to get to the next level, sometimes, we must be uncomfortable. Ask yourself, "Am I comfortable with being comfortable?"

Here are some tips to help you transition out of your comfort zones:
- Try a new recipe that includes a different type of herb that you have never tasted.
- Try a new dish when you go out to eat.
- Be open to new things that promote physical, mental, and spiritual health.

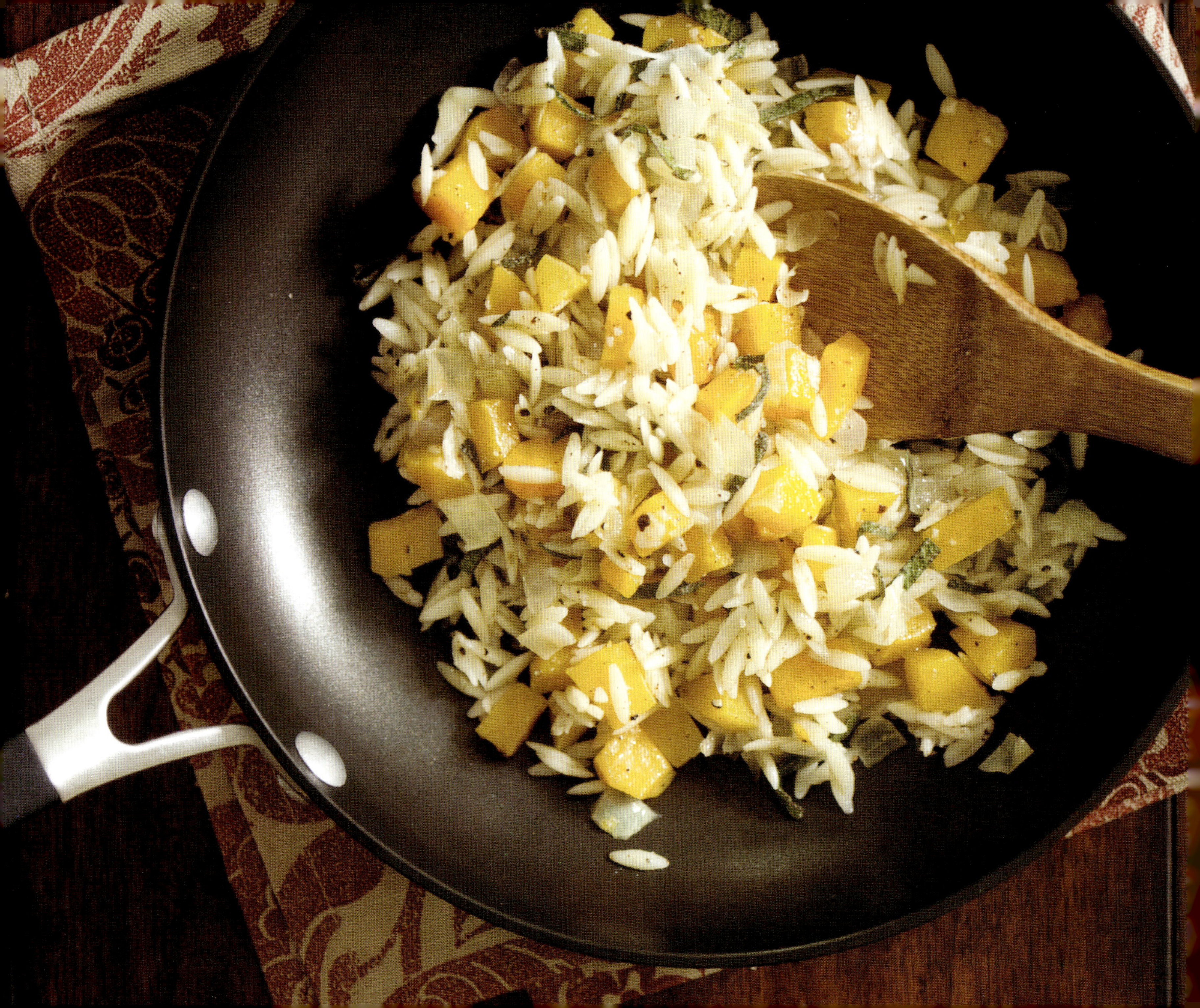

the aha moment

butternut squash orzo w/sage

ingredients:

3 tbsp unsalted butter

1 tbsp extra virgin olive oil

1 medium onion, chopped

2 cloves garlic, minced

3 cups butternut squash, peeled and cubed

4 cups low sodium chicken broth

1 cup orzo pasta (whole wheat, optional)

½ cup freshly grated Parmesan or Parmigiano Reggiano cheese

2 tbsp fresh sage, chopped

Kosher salt & cracked black pepper to taste

Dash of nutmeg

directions:

In a skillet pan, melt butter with olive oil over medium-high heat. Add onion and cook for about 5-6 minutes, or until tender. Add garlic and cook for 30 seconds. Add squash and stir. While stirring your squash, add ½ cup vegetable broth and simmer over medium heat until liquid is absorbed and squash is tender.

In a separate pot, bring the remaining broth to a boil. Add orzo and cook for about 8 minutes, until al dente. Now is a good time to read Are You Comfortable with Being Comfortable (page 46). After 8 minutes, drain any excess liquid. Combine squash mixture with orzo and heat together for a few minutes, until the squash is tender. Pour into bowl and toss with sage and cheese. Add salt, pepper and nutmeg. Serve, eat and enjoy!

Serves 4
Calories 203; Fat 13g; Saturated Fat 7g; Carbohydrates 17g; Protein 5g; Sodium 446mg; Fiber 4g

chef tianna's tips:

This dish is best served with kale or collard greens and roasted chicken cooked with fresh herbs (sage or basil). You can use sage or basil for the orzo.

If you are cooking for vegetarians, use a low sodium vegetable broth.

strength in the struggle

the aha moment

Sometimes we wonder, "Why am I struggling?" Whether you believe it or not, there is strength in the struggle. We all tend to struggle with our eating habits and fitness routines. It's about attitude adjustments. You have to constantly renew your mind about your eating habits and exercising. I know I do. We also give the excuse, "I don't have time to exercise!" You need to make the time. Ask yourself, "Do I have time to take care of me?" It involves hard work, discipline and sacrifice. We need to believe it, do it, and expect the rewards that will surely come. There are days when I don't feel like exercising. I do it because my body needs it. Sometimes there are days when I want to just eat a hot dog, french fries, a burger, pizza or just have some chips. I will eat the whole bag of chips, especially if I am in the *red zone*. There is nothing like that salty taste. I strive to keep in focus that it's okay to treat myself but not to go crazy with it. I know I need a treat day, don't you? I know it can be unsettling sometimes because we tend to find comfort in food, especially when we are dealing with personal issues. Find the strength within your spirit not to overindulge and pick one day or time when you will give yourself permission to splurge. We eat to live. We shouldn't live to eat. Now, I'm not saying that you should not enjoy your food. Just be sensible with the choices and portions and always do some form of exercise to maintain overall health.

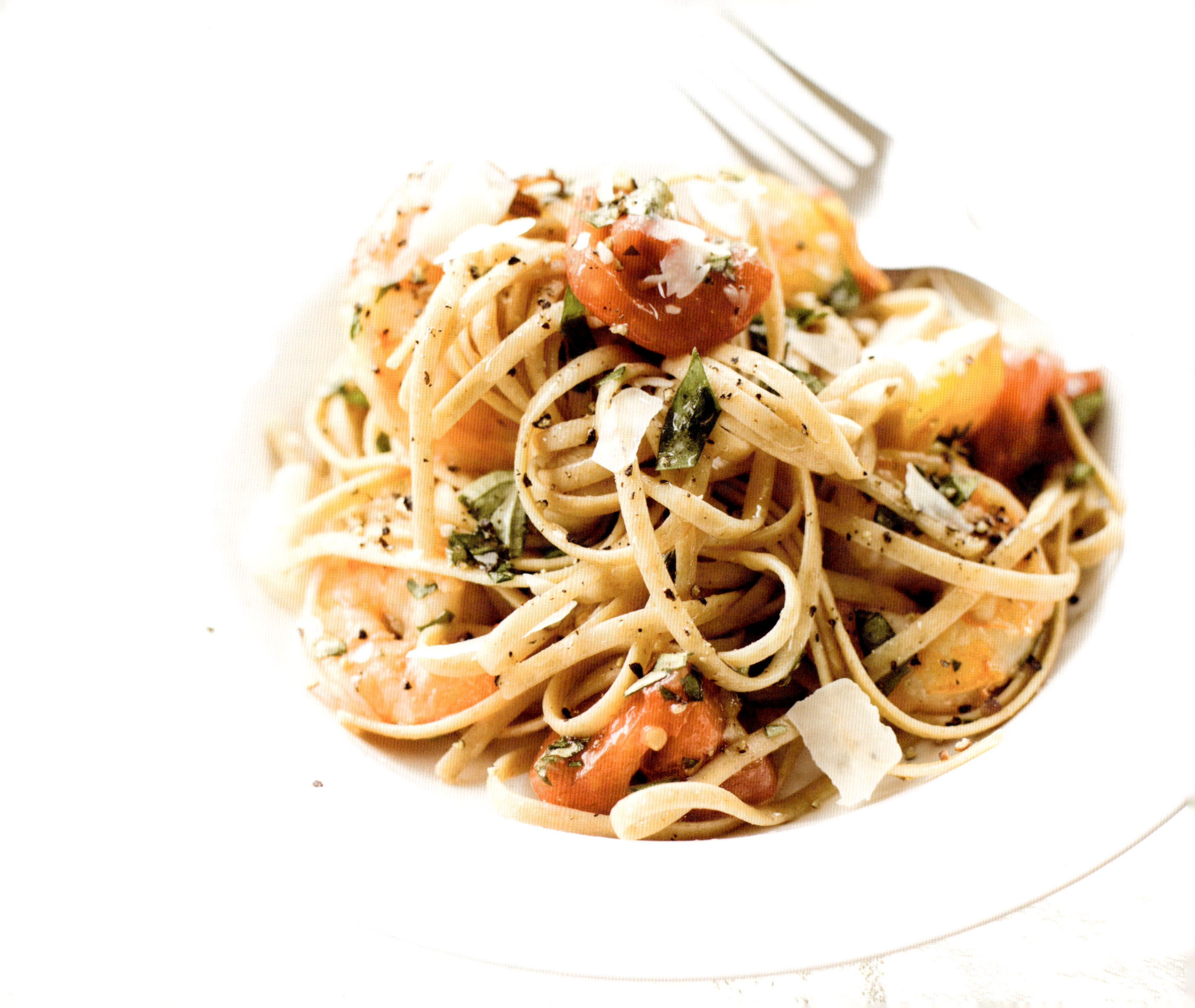

the aha moment

whole wheat linguine w/ shrimp, heirloom tomatoes & basil

ingredients:

3 garlic cloves, minced

3 tbsp olive oil

½ cup fresh basil leaves

1 cup heirloom tomatoes

1 lb shrimp, peeled & deveined

½ tsp kosher salt & black pepper

12 oz uncooked whole-wheat linguine

2 oz (¾ cup) Parmesan cheese, finely grated

directions:

In a large skillet, sauté minced garlic for 20-30 seconds in pan with olive oil over medium heat. Add shrimp, sauté and then add tomatoes (cut in half), salt and pepper. Once the shrimp are pink and tomatoes start to get tender, add fresh basil. In a large pot add water until about ¾ filled. Bring to a boil. Add the linguine and cook until al dente or until tender, yet with texture. (See package for cooking time.) Drain pasta thoroughly. Add linguine to the skillet with the shrimp, tomato, and basil. Toss gently until noodles are coated. After placing on a plate, top with fresh Parmesan cheese. While eating and enjoying this meal, take the time to reflect on how you have found Strength in the Struggle.

Serves 6
Calories 248; Fat 11g; Saturated Fat 3g; Carbohydrates 9.5; Protein 26.5g; Sodium 874mg; Fiber 2g

chef tianna's tips:

This dish is best served with a caesar salad.
Grape or cherry tomatoes can be substituted for heirloom tomatoes.

fresh start

dig deep inside of you

fresh start

When I was a little girl, my mother loved buying me gifts with my name on them, especially when she went out of town with my dad on his business trips. There was one problem. There was never anything with the name, "Tianna." As a result, my mom used my middle name, "Michelle." That usage made shopping successful for my mom. There was a bigger plan, however, for my name, such as "Princess Tiana," as in the movie The Princess and the Frog. Princess Tiana is the first African American Disney character. Wow, even now at my age, my mom is buying items imprinted with the name "Princess Tiana." I just love it!

I love the movie, The Princess and the Frog. What was so engaging about the movie is that I felt like the story was about me, and that a lot of people can relate to it. In life, we have to dig deeper. What's most meaningful is not on the exterior but on the interior. In some form or manner, everything that we put inside of us reflects on the outside of us. Sometimes, we have the tendency not to recognize how great we are or how deep our love goes as we care and share. That's why I say that it starts within. In the movie, Princess Tiana proclaimed that she would NEVER, EVER, EVER kiss a frog. Well, that night of the Ball, in desperation, she kissed the frog and turned into a frog herself! YIKES! Princess Tiana ended up getting more than she bargained for. But, in the end, she was able to respect the life of a frog. Also, Princes Tiana learned to dig deep within herself where she found self-love and self-worth. Her lessons taught her, even more, how to share love and worth in relationships.

Regarding our lifestyles, when it comes to our choices, remember the interior actions begin the exterior motions. Want to change your eating habits and start exercising and, most importantly, be consistent with it? Then you know what? It starts within. You have what it takes – we all do. There is a Princess Tiana in many of us. We just have to be confident that we will rise to the top. So, dig deep and know that, you, too, are more than a frog!

fresh start

roasted brussel sprouts

ingredients:

1 ½ lbs fresh brussel sprouts

3 tbsp extra virgin olive oil

1 tsp kosher salt

1 tsp freshly ground black pepper

2 tbsp sherry vinegar

2 tbsp dry white wine

2 tsp brown sugar

1 tbsp unsalted butter

directions:

Preheat oven to 400ºF. Rinse the brussel sprouts. Cut the sprouts in halves. Mix them in a bowl with olive oil, salt and pepper, sherry vinegar, wine and brown sugar. Pour them onto a sheet pan, add butter. Cover with aluminum foil and roast for 20 minutes. This is a good time to Dig Deep Inside of You to discover the love you have for your family and self in order to make healthy choices.

Remove the cover and continue to roast for another 10 minutes, until crisp on the outside and tender on the inside. Shake the pan from time to time. Sprinkle with more kosher salt if needed and serve immediately.

Serves 4

Calories 188; Fat 10g; Saturated Fat 2g; Carbohydrates 21g; Protein 5g; Sodium 47mg; Fiber 6.5g

chef tianna's tips:

This dish is great with baked chicken and roasted potatoes.

fresh start

twice baked sweet potatoes

ingredients:

4 medium-size sweet potatoes

1 tbsp of extra virgin olive oil

1 tbsp of fresh sage, chopped

1-2 shallots, minced

1-2 tbsp of fresh shredded/ shaved Parmesan cheese

Kosher salt & freshly ground black pepper

directions:

Preheat oven to 375ºF. Cut sweet potatoes in halves. Place sweet potatoes on sheet tray, cover with aluminum foil and bake for 1 hour or until soft. Let potatoes cool then, using a spoon, scoop out the flesh and place in a medium sized bowl, reserving the skins. In another bowl, add shallots, sage, parmesan cheese, and olive oil. Add the mixture to the sweet potato flesh and fold in completely. Add salt, black pepper, and mix. Add the filling back to the potato skins and place on a half sheet tray. Bake for 15 minutes or until golden brown. As you dig deep into your delicious sweet potatoes, Dig Deep Inside of You too.

Serves 4
Calories 292; Fat 18g; Saturated Fat 2.5g; Carbohydrates 12g; Protein 21g; Sodium 324mg; Fiber 2g

chef tianna's tips:

For all of my cheese lovers, it's okay to add extra cheese; it's low in carbohydrates. Sweet potatoes are a great complex carbohydrate to add to your dishes. This recipe is great for folks, like me, who are not big sweet eaters. It's sweet but yet savory by using fresh sage. Also, basil is another herb that you can add to give it a great flavor. Sweet potato is one of the greatest vegetables you can eat and is a part of the all star team of great vegetables.

If you want to make your own ravioli stuffing let me recommend using the same ingredients in this recipe and maybe add another cheese like mascarpone or ricotta cheese. Then stuff this mixture inside the ravioli. It's delicious!

forgiveness

fresh start

Regularly, we battle with challenges to forgive. It can be even harder to forgive ourselves. It is difficult to re-play how we faltered and failed. What we need to do is forgive ourselves and others, and make the necessary amends in order to move forward successfully.

We tend to be very unforgiving with ourselves when it comes to our diet and exercising. If we started off right for the first few weeks and then slipped up, immediately, we start chastising ourselves. That can lead to us giving in to attitudes of defeat, which can lead to choices of neglecting our healthy commitments. STOP!! Resist the urges to do that to yourself. Recently, I was watching a couple of ladies I know use a diet that is really working for them. Not only are they encouraging themselves, but others, as well. That is so important. Like we say, folks lead by example.

When we have what we call "cheat" days, sometimes we get a little discouraged. You just have to say, "Remember it's in the past. It doesn't matter." Keep at it until you get it right. Be mindful that what might work for others may not work for you. Everybody is different and responds differently to diet and exercise, as well as to other lifestyle changes. You have to figure out what works for you. AND never give up. When you do miss your mark, forgive yourself, re-group, and move forward.

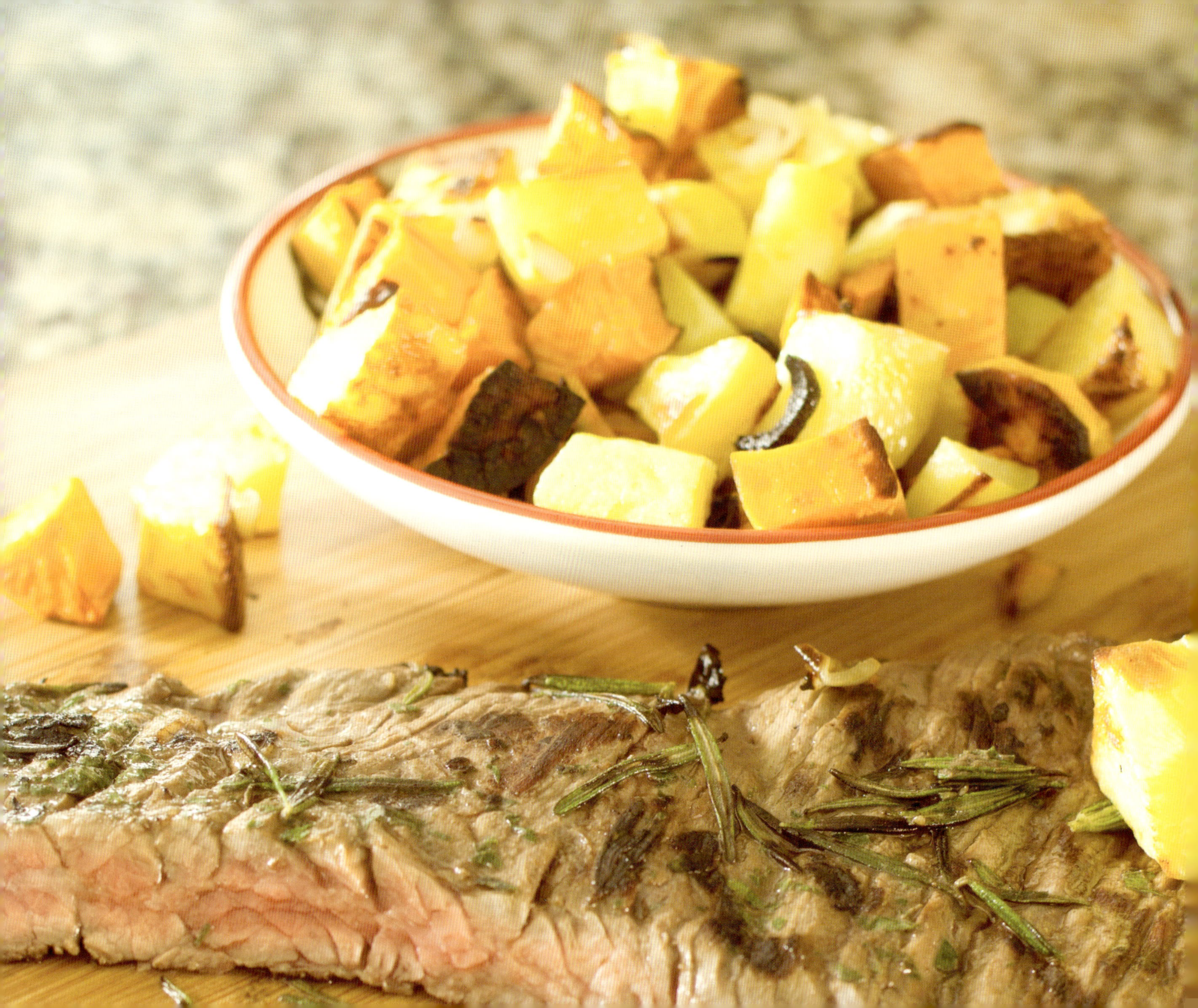

fresh start

roasted sweet & white potatoes w/ shallots & sage

ingredients:

3 medium size white, or Yukon Gold potatoes, cut into inch cubes

3 medium size sweet potatoes, cut into ¾ inch cubes

¼ cup sunflower oil

1 shallot, chopped

2 tbsp fresh sage, chopped

Kosher salt & cracked black pepper

directions:

Preheat oven to 425°F. Combine all ingredients in large bowl; toss to coat. Spread mixture in single layer on a large rimmed baking sheet. For about 30 minutes, roast potatoes until they are tender and brown around edges. Stir occasionally. While waiting, this would be a good time to read Forgiveness (page 60). Once the potatoes are done, serve immediately. Eat and enjoy!

Serves 6
Calories: 287 Fat 13.75g; Saturated Fat 1.5g; Carbohydrates 37.7g; Protein 4.8g; Sodium 365mg; Fiber 6.25g

chef tianna's tips:

For all of my meat and potato eaters out there, this dish is best served with the Grilled Tuscan Skirt Steak (page 33).

if there's a will,
there's a way!

fresh start

In a recent Bible study, we discussed God's will and what was also discussed was the old saying, "If there's a will, there's a way." I asked my group if we honestly know what we are saying when we make that statement? Or, are we just making a statement because it sounds like the right thing to say, without any meaning or actual belief in what we are saying? The statement is a cliché, but it is so true in life. IF THERE'S A WILL, THERE'S DEFINITELY A WAY.

When it comes to having and/or maintaining a healthy lifestyle, if there's a will, there's a way. When it comes to eating properly and exercising, you have to be willing to want a healthier lifestyle. It has to be within you. It's like having the fight inside of you saying, "Get up, go exercise. It's a beautiful day outside to walk, bike or run." Instead of eating at a fast food establishment because it is fast and cheap, why don't you go home and prepare a healthy meal.

When I was younger, I would ask my dad to stop at this particular fast food place that we would pass by on the way home. He would answer, "No, I am going to go home and fix you a real hamburger." I'm so thankful that my father did that for me. But as a young child, his answer crushed me because I wasn't mature enough then to appreciate the wisdom in his words and actions. NOW, I know what he meant. My father made sure that his daughter ate quality food.

I know what you are saying, "Tianna, I'm tired when I get home. I have to help my kids with their homework. I do not have time to exercise. I am too tired." The key is that you have to be willing. Try to plan your day to fit in cooking dinner and going for a walk. I know it is challenging because life definitely throws curve balls, but remember if there's a will, there's a way. Embrace the freedom in that truth. Keep in mind that we all have fight in us. So, let's fight the good fight of faith and be willing to make choices that result in positive changes to improve our lifestyles. Healthy adjustments gain rewards for our souls, our minds and our bodies.

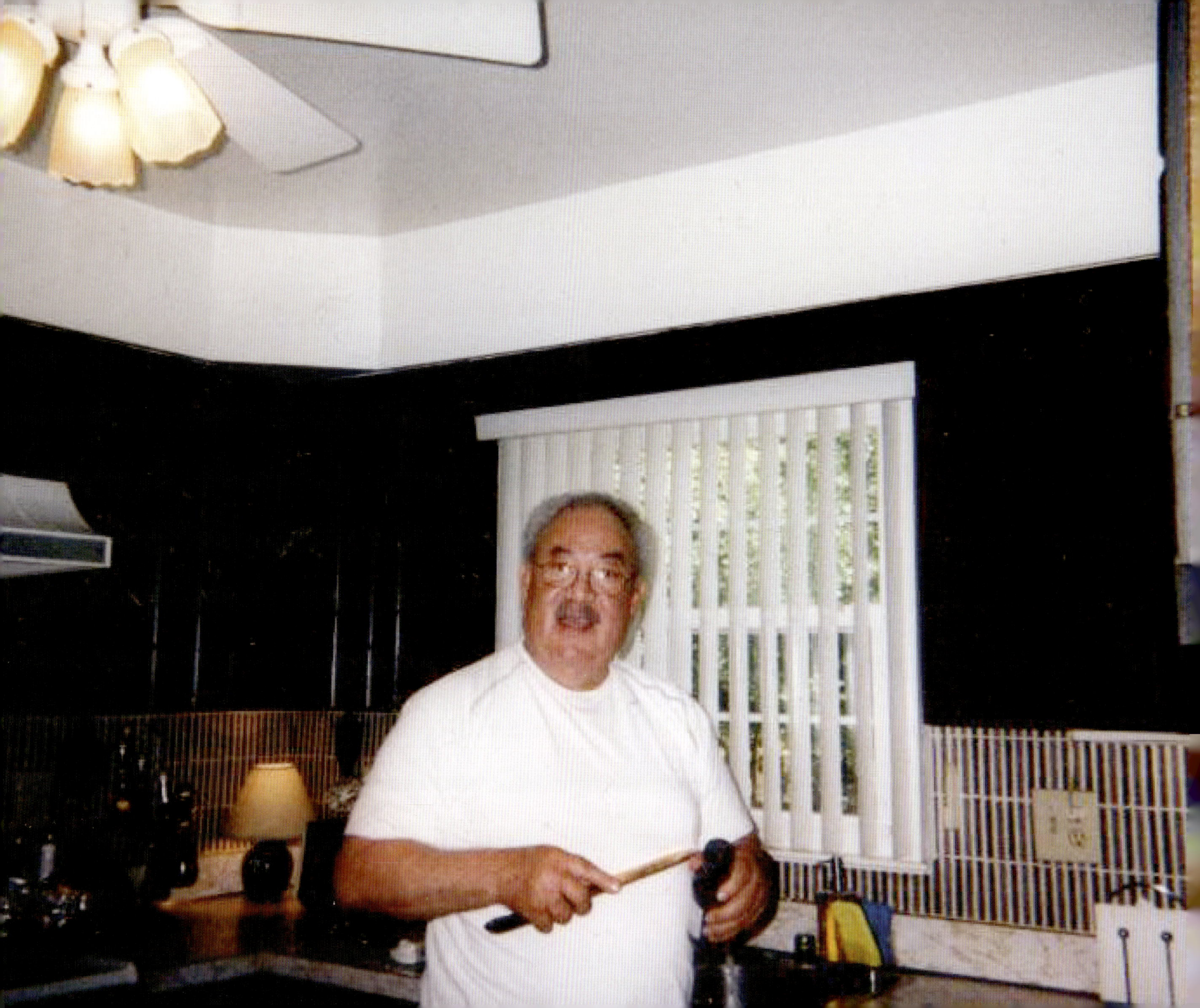

fresh start

the real deal phil burger

ingredients:

1 ⅓ lb of lean ground beef

6oz blue cheese, crumbled

2 scallions, chopped

Salt & pepper

2 tbsp of Worcestershire sauce

Olive oil, for drizzling

Fresh spinach or arugula leaves

½ red medium size onion, sliced

1 tomato, sliced

4 whole wheat buns

directions:

Burgers

Combine ground beef, salt and pepper, 2 tbsp Worcestershire sauce, and 1 tbsp of olive oil in a bowl. Form into 4 large patties. Make a small indentation in the center of each patty, place 1 tbsp of crumbled blue cheese in it, and press the beef up and around, to cover it. Brush grill with olive oil and cook patties 8 to 10 minutes on each side.

Bun

Split the bun and toast on the grill, in the oven, and/or toaster oven until golden. Place a burger on the bottom of the bun. Top with tomato, lettuce, spinach and a slice of red onion. Add several leaves of spinach/arugula, and the remaining bread.

Serves 4

Calories 361; Fat 14g; Saturated Fat 6g; Carbohydrates 25g; Protein 32g; Sodium 552mg; Fiber 3g

chef tianna's tips:

For all of those who don't eat red meats, you can substitute with lean ground turkey.
If using turkey, be sure to make sure the burger is completely done.
Best served with Roasted Sweet and White Potatoes w/Shallots and Sage (page 63).

starting over

fresh start

The one thing I love about the New Year, it is a reminder that we can start over. You can start over by renewing your mind and spirit, making healthier food choices, being consistent with your exercising, building new relationships, finding a new career and overall, having a blast as you pursue your dreams. There are so many opportunities to start over. Every day when you wake up you are blessed with another opportunity to begin fresh. Set your goals and go for it! When it comes to adopting a healthier eating lifestyle, as you journey throughout this year and beyond, resist the urge to join typical resolution fads and attitudes. Embrace healthier living. Go for the gusto! Just do it!

When, occasionally, your plans unravel, don't be discouraged. Determine that you will get there. Remember, you're in it to win it! So what, you ate a couple of things that you shouldn't have eaten–start over. So what you didn't exercise today–start over and do it tomorrow. Remember, every day we get another chance to start over. You don't have to wait until a new year to begin fresh–do it today!

fresh start

breakfast wrap

ingredients:

- 3 egg whites or ½ cup egg white substitute
- 8-inch whole-wheat tortilla wrap
- 3 slices cooked turkey or regular bacon
- 1 tbsp reduced fat cheddar cheese, shredded
- 2 tbsp tomatoes, diced
- 4 fresh spinach leaves
- Kosher salt & black pepper
- Olive oil non stick spray

directions:

Whisk egg whites together in a small bowl and combine shredded cheese. Spray olive oil non stick spray in skillet. Cook eggs and cheese mixture in a small nonstick skillet until reaching desired consistency. Add salt and pepper to taste. To put together the wrap, layer the ingredients horizontally across the middle of a tortilla as follows: one quarter of the scrambled eggs mixture, diced tomatoes, strips of bacon, and spinach leaves. Roll up the wrap. If you yielded to temptation yesterday, this is a great day to start over. Eat and enjoy!

Serves 1

Calories 186; Fat 4g; Saturated Fat 1g; Carbohydrates 18g; Protein 19g; Sodium 667mg; Fiber 5g

chef tianna's tips:

This is best served with a seasonal fruit salad. You can double the recipe to serve more as desired.

fresh start

watermelon w/ arugula & mint vinaigrette

ingredients:

1 pound watermelon flesh, chopped and cubed

¼ cup red wine vinegar

1 tbsp honey

2 tbsp of fresh mint, chopped

½ cup extra-virgin olive oil

1 sweet onion

4 ounces fat free feta cheese crumbled

1 bundle fresh arugula

½ cup of pine nuts, toasted

Salt & pepper to taste

Fresh lemon juice

directions:

Vinaigrette
To prepare the vinaigrette, combine vinegar, honey, lemon juice, salt and pepper and whisk together. In a thin stream, whisking constantly add the oil until incorporated. Add the chopped mint, taste and adjust seasoning. Set aside.

Salad
Cut the flesh from the melon and cut into bite size pieces, removing and discarding the seeds, and set aside. Peel and slice the onion into rings. In a large bowl, combine the melon, onion, feta, pine nut and arugula. Pour the dressing over the salad mixture and toss gently until everything is coated and evenly mixed. To serve, divide salad among individual plates and garnish with mint leaves. Eat and enjoy.

Serves 6

Salad: Calories 176; Fat 12g; Saturated Fat 3.5g; Carbohydrates 13.5g; Protein 6g; Sodium 226mg; Fiber 1.8g

Dressing: Calories 173; Fat 18 g; Saturated Fat 2.5g; Carbohydrates 3g; Sodium 2mg

chef tianna's tips:

If pine nuts are not in season, use pumpkin or sunflower seeds; something with texture.
This is best served with Tilapia or Skirt Steak. Arugula is a year round green vegetable.

letting go is a process

fresh start

Is letting go a process? The answer is YES!! In life, there are seasons when we let go of jobs, loved ones, marriages, relationships, children, anger, and an assortment of situations and/or circumstances. It can be difficult to let go but, once you do, you are free and the best is yet to come. Why is it so hard to let go? Is it because we fear the unknown and think that this is as good as it gets? When it comes to adopting a healthier lifestyle, letting go of bad eating habits is a process. I think sometimes we believe we can just STOP cold turkey from consuming certain foods and drinks, for example, sodas. If you drink sodas every day, try to limit your consumption to three times a week. Increase your water intake. If you crave carbonation, drink seltzer water; it is a healthier choice than soda.

In determing to eliminate unwise food selections, it can help to change our habits and to let things go gradually. I am certain there were times when you have gone to a fast-food restaurant and purchased the crispy chicken sandwich. In the future, instead, select the grilled chicken sandwich on a whole wheat bun. Again, change is a process. When you are preparing dishes, you may be tempted to use vegetable oil, salted butter or whole milk. Well, how about substituting the vegetable oil with olive oil, the salted butter with unsalted butter, and the whole milk with fat free or 2% milk? Don't be discouraged. As you gradually adapt, you'll start to notice the rewards for your choices to adopt healthier eating habits. Know that, progressively, it gets better. Yes, you will be blessed with the benefits of spiritual, mental, and physical health.

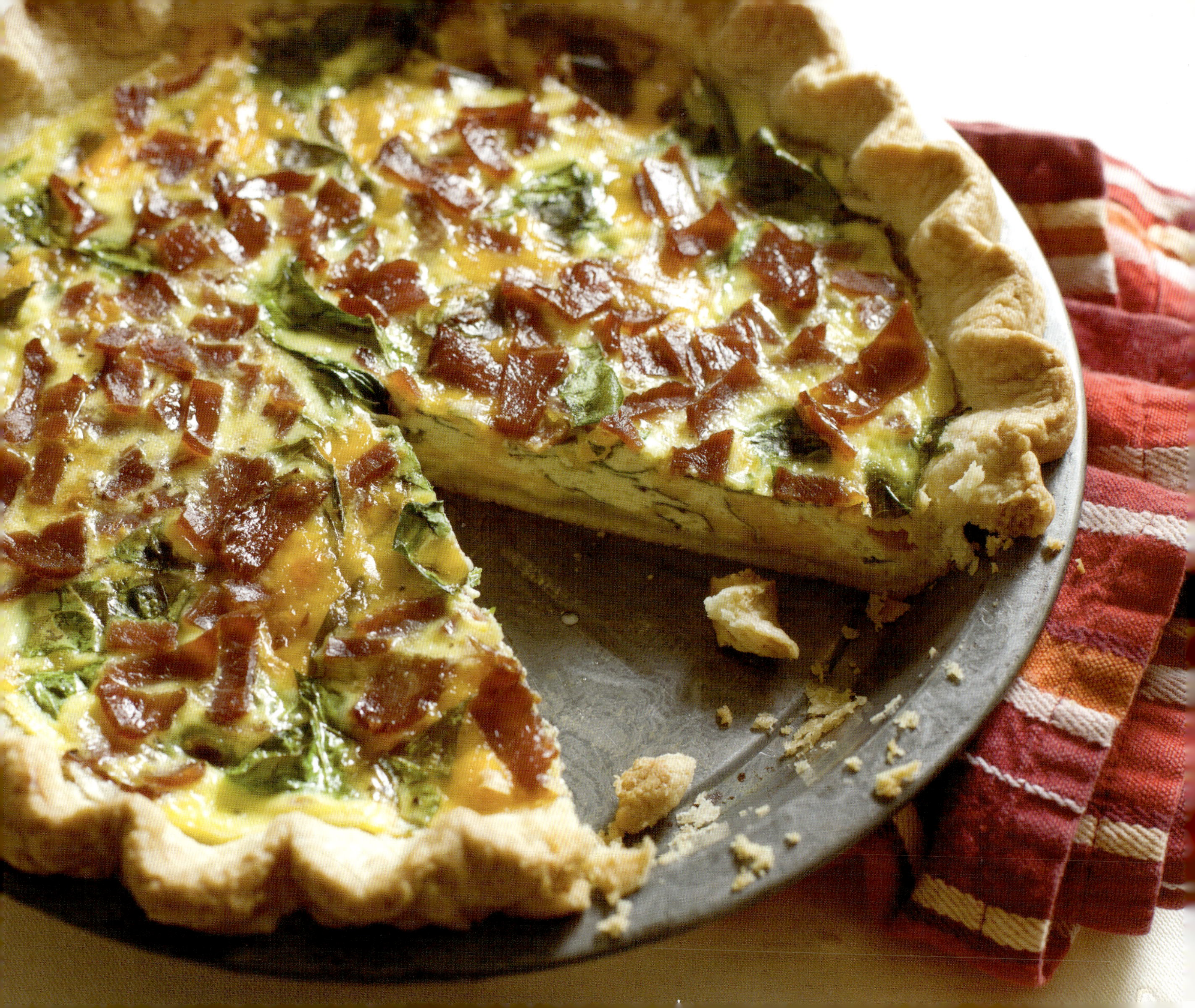

fresh start

brunch quiche

ingredients:

6 slices of turkey or pork bacon

1 regular 9-inch pie crust

1 cup fresh spinach

3 eggs

1 cup of 2% milk

2 tbsp shallots, minced

1 cup reduced fat sharp cheddar cheese

Kosher salt & cracked black pepper

directions:

Heat your oven to 425°F – 450°F high broil. Place bacon on cooking sheet with foil (to make it easy to clean up). Cook for about 8 minutes or until bacon is nice and crispy. Drain on paper towel. Set aside. Reset oven to 375°F. Place crust on baking sheet. Bake 5-7 minutes or until very light golden brown. If bubbles form, gently press with back of wooden spoon.

Meanwhile, beat eggs and milk in medium bowl. Stir in cheese, spinach, shallots and seasonings. Pour into crust. Sprinkle with bacon. Bake 25-30 minutes or until filling is browned. While enjoying this healthy quiche, read Letting Go Is a Process (page 72) and discuss with your family.

Serves 6
Calories 271; Fat 16g; Saturated Fat 5g; Carbohydrates 17g; Protein 13g; Sodium 501mg; Fiber 1g

chef tianna's tips:

You can be creative with this quiche by adding leftover vegetables or your choice of meats (ham, chicken, or sausage), or seafood (crab, shrimp or salmon).

renewing your mind

fresh start

Usually, we have annual rituals on how we plan to improve, and what we intentionally do or cease to do to change our lives. We start off by making resolutions to: lose weight, change exercise routines, eat better, quit smoking, save money, improve personal budgets, find another job, go to school, stop drinking, pursue dreams, go to church, start a hobby, meet a great mate, stop cursing, stay positive, spend more time with family, take more vacations, buy a house, etc. Our list goes on and on. I ask myself and others, "Do we really stick to our declared resolutions?" More often than not, the answer is NO, not really. Why? We don't stick to our resolutions because in order to make necessary adjustments, we have to change our attitudes, and renew our minds. We have to change the way we perceive things. Everything starts from within us. By changing our attitudes, eventually our minds become renewed. During this process, there may be times we may feel like things are not happening quickly enough. We may get frustrated with the process and become tempted to cheat. Do not give up. STAY THE COURSE!

CHANGE was his theme word when Barack Obama was on the campaign trail for his first presidential run. His emphasis was on change within us. We must change our attitudes and set our minds on higher standards.

In order to change, determination and perseverance should be in the mix when it comes to eating healthy and exercising. Anything worthwhile requires diligence and sacrifice. You have heard the statements: "I don't like to sweat; my hair gets messed up. I don't like vegetables. I don't like water. It's hard. I don't have time." Defeated mindsets need to be renewed! When folks make such excuses, it isn't helpful for positive goal achievement. I know because I've made some of the same excuses; however, to cause change in my own life, I had to renew my mind and adjust the way that I perceived things. My question for you today is, "Are you changing your attitude toward eating properly and exercising?" Don't talk about change or desire to change–DO change. Every day, let's resolve to live right by forsaking our old ways of thinking. Let's be open to the renewing of our minds and let's manifest healthy choices throughout the year and beyond. CHANGE is:

C – Creating
H – Healthy
A – Attitude towards
N – New
G – Goals and
E – Expectations

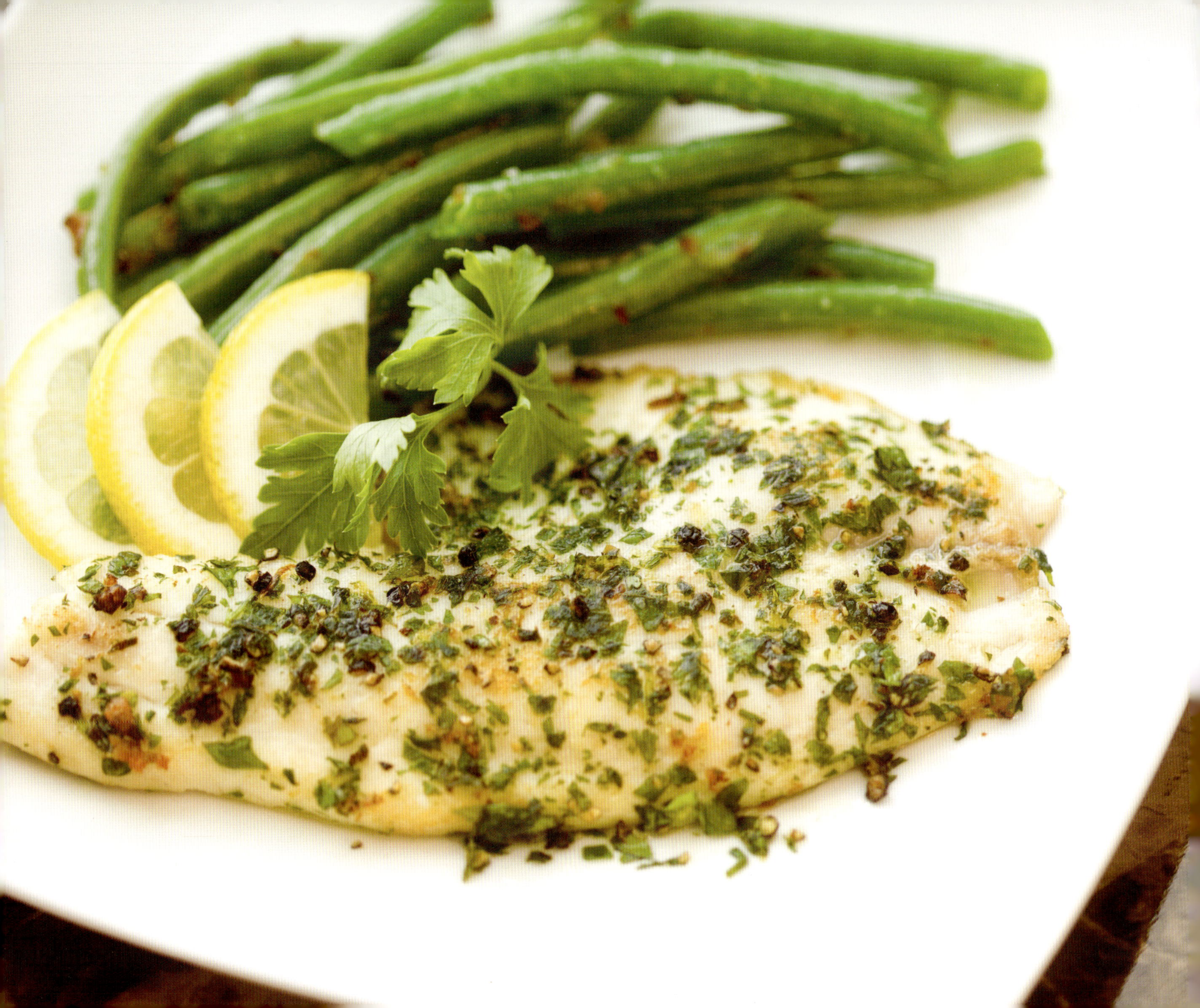

fresh start

lemon herbed tilapia

ingredients:

4 skinless tilapia fillets (about 4oz each)

1 tbsp fresh lemon juice

¼ tsp lemon zest

¼ cup each chopped fresh herbs (parsley, cilantro, thyme)

Kosher salt & cracked black pepper

2 tbsp extra-virgin olive oil

directions:

Mix the herbs and lemon zest on a plate. Sprinkle the fillets with salt and pepper and coat both sides of each fillet with herbs, pressing them on so that they adhere to fish.

In a large (12-inch) nonstick skillet, heat the oil over medium heat until hot. Cook the tilapia until the flesh is opaque and just cooked through, about 2 minutes on each side. Cut into the thick part of a fillet to check doness. Slice lemon into quarters. Serve the tilapia with the lemon quarters. Start Renewing Your Mind. You will see positive results.

Serves 4
Calories 143; Fat 8.25g; Saturated Fat 1.5g; Carbohydrates .5g; Protein 17.2g; Sodium 84mg; Fiber .25g

chef tianna's tips:

This dish is best served with linguine that has been tossed in olive oil and REAL unsalted butter along with a side of green beans or broccolini.

keeping it moving

loving yourself
the healthy way

keeping it moving

I have heard it said that "the greatest love of all is loving yourself." But why is it one of the hardest things to do? It takes sacrifice and discipline to take care of you. You may think, "I don't feel like getting up at 4 or 5 a.m. to exercise. I have kids. I'm in school. I have to work. I don't have enough time." You're not alone. There are days when I don't feel like eating a salad, and I just want a burger, especially when I am in the red zone. There are times when I wake up at 4 a.m. to exercise and don't want to leave the bed. That little voice inside, however, says get up, do it, handle your business. I know it's hard but you have to do it for yourself.

Remember, YOU are important and the only way you can be beneficial to anything or anyone is if you take care of yourself. You can't give something that you don't possess. That's why the key to having a healthy family starts within your heart, your mind and your spirit. Eventually, your healthy lifestyle will affect the people around you. Parents, if your children notice you taking care of yourself and demonstrating confidence in yourself when it comes to eating right and exercising, they will likely emulate your positive actions. Remember, we lead by example. Tell yourself, "I can live a healthier lifestyle!"

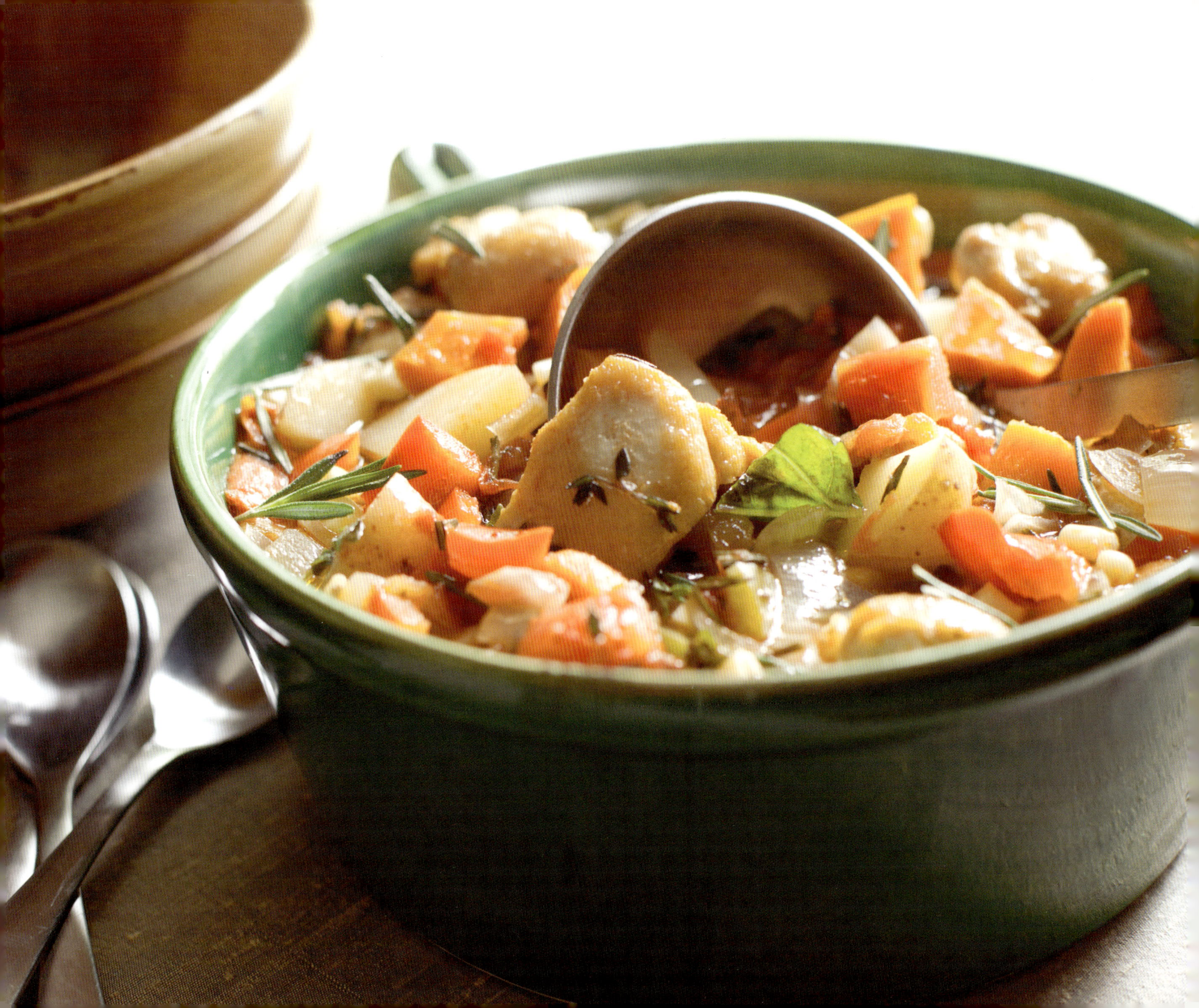

keeping it moving

chicken stew

ingredients:

- 2 pounds boneless, skinless chicken thighs
- 1 medium onion, cut into ½ inch slices
- 1 carrot peeled, cut into bite size pieces
- Salt & freshly ground black pepper
- 1 red bell pepper, chopped
- 1 green bell pepper, chopped
- 1 cup red potatoes, chopped
- ½ cup canned corn, drained
- ½ cup basil leaves, torn into pieces
- 2 ½ cups low sodium chicken broth
- 2 cloves garlic, minced
- 2 tbsp olive oil
- 1 can tomatoes, diced
- 2 sprigs fresh rosemary
- 2 tbsp fresh thyme

directions:

Heat the oil in a heavy 5 ½-quart saucepan over medium heat. Add the red and green bell peppers, carrot, potatoes and onions. Sauté the vegetables until the onions are translucent, about 5 minutes. Season with salt and black pepper, to taste; however, maintain a healthy amount. Stir in the diced tomatoes with their juices, chicken broth, basil, rosemary, and thyme. Reduce heat to a medium-low simmer. Heat a skillet over medium-high heat. Season chicken with salt, pepper and thyme. Put chicken in pan until both sides are a light brown. Remove chicken from skillet and place in saucepan. Simmer gently uncovered until the chicken is almost cooked through, turning the chicken thighs over and stirring the mixture occasionally, about 25 - 30 minutes. Transfer the chicken thighs to a work surface and cool for 5 minutes. Shred or cut the chicken into bite-size pieces. Return the chicken meat to the stew. Bring the stew to a simmer. Season with salt and pepper to taste. This is a good time for an evaluation: Are You Loving Yourself the Health Way?

Serves 4-6
Calories 228; Fat 11g; Saturated Fat 2.5g; Carbohydrates 14g; Protein 17g; Sodium 634mg; Fiber 3.1g

chef tianna's tips:

If you are slow cooking in a crock pot you can combine all ingredients, cover and cook on low 6 to 8 hours, until chicken is done and vegetables are tender. This dish is best served with a mixed green salad.

This is another great dish to freeze in a Ziploc bag and save to eat later.

what are we feeding
our children?

keeping it moving

One morning I got in line to buy water at my neighborhood 7 Eleven. As I stood in line, I saw a woman with her son. I just happened to glance and notice that she was purchasing the following items:
- Gatorade
- Doritos
- Slim Jim
- Chicken wings
- Dole fruit cup
- Lunchable

Now, I ask you, what was wrong with that picture? I wanted, so badly, to say something. Nothing in those selections was healthy for her son. He is a growing young boy and there was nothing nutritional in that lunch menu for him. Okay, maybe the fruit cup, but many fruit cups are drenched in high fructose corn syrup. We are going at such hectic paces that we are now shopping at 7 Eleven for our children's lunches. Come on family, we have got to be better than that. So much of that food is high in sodium and loaded with sugar. Granted, that boy may have burned it off in camp or elsewhere. I don't know. These are some reasons why our children are now suffering from obesity, which leads to diabetes, cancer and high blood pressure. We have to be more accountable!

What are we doing to promote healthy food choices for our children? Thinking quick and cheap is not the answer. If we don't change our attitudes, we and they are going to pay later! These are not sufficient well-balanced meals for our kids. The nonsense has to stop! My questions are: "Do we not have time anymore? Are we too busy? Are we not prioritizing? Do we just not know what to do?" Well, I have some tips that I believe can assist you with packing your children healthy lunches. Here are some healthy choices:
- Prepare sandwiches with whole wheat bread; however, if your child has gluten or allergy issues there are other healthy breads available.
- Include fresh fruit – to save money, buy seasonal. We all need a certain amount of fruits and vegetables daily.
- Raw carrots, celery, broccoli w/dip – Kids love to dip!
- Water or some type of fresh juice–a real juice–no Gatorade or sodas; they can rot children's teeth and provide no nutritional benefit.
- Whole Grain/Pumpernickel pretzels or kettle cooked chips (Read the nutritional information on bags.)

Again, I know that life has varied issues; however, if we don't make wise choices, we will pay later. So, please, take time to plan, prepare and pack your children healthy lunches. This is what First Lady, Michelle Obama, is promoting in our nation. Let's act on it by being accountable for ourselves, families and our communities. Let's share our concerns and information about the benefits of the practice of balanced diets joined with an exercise plan in which we regularly engage.

keeping it moving

crunchy cornflake chicken tenders

ingredients:

1 lb. chicken tenders or breast

2 cups Cornflakes (Kellogg's)

1 tsp salt

½ tsp garlic powder

1 tsp black pepper

½ tsp fresh sage, chopped

½ tsp fresh thyme, chopped

1 large egg, beaten

½ cup low fat buttermilk

Canola/olive oil spray

directions:

Preheat oven to 400ºF. Line a baking sheet tray with foil and spray it with oil. Season chicken with salt, pepper, garlic powder, sage and thyme. Place the cereal and all of the seasonings in a Ziploc bag and crush with a rolling pin OR place in a food processor until mixture is the size of breadcrumbs. Pour breadcrumb mixture onto a plate. Put egg and buttermilk in a bowl and whisk to combine.

Dip chicken tenders in buttermilk/egg mixture and then roll in cornflakes, coating the chicken completely. Place the chicken tenders on the sheet tray and lightly spray them with oil. Bake for 16-20 minutes or until done. Now there should be no questions on What We Are Feeding Our Children.

Serves 6

Calories 107; Fat 7g; Saturated Fat 4g; Carbohydrates 3g; Protein 4g; Sodium 121mg; Fiber 1.2g

chef tianna's tips:

For kids, chicken fingers are best served with broccoli or Mac and cheese.
This is a great way to prep and freeze for another day. No more purchasing frozen chicken strips; now you have your own frozen healthy chicken fingers.

keeping it moving

apple salsa & brie puff pastry

ingredients:

2 tbsp cider vinegar

1 tsp olive oil

½ tsp honey

Salt & pepper to taste

1 tart apple, peeled, cored & finely diced (about 2 cups)

½ red bell pepper, finely chopped

½ red onion or shallot, finely chopped

Small handful fresh cilantro, finely chopped

1 pkg Pepperidge Farm Puff Pastry Sheets (about 2 sheets)

½ pound brie cheese, rind removed

directions:

Apple Salsa

Stir together vinegar, oil and honey. Season with salt and pepper. In medium bowl, add apple, bell pepper, onion and cilantro and toss to combine. Add dressing to mixture in the bowl and stir to coat.

Brie Puff Pastry

Cut each pastry sheet into 12 (3") squares. Press squares into 3" muffin pan cups. Place in about 2 tsp of cheese in the middle of the puff pastry and then mound a heaping teaspoon of salsa in the middle of the puff pastry and fold the 4 sides toward the middle and bake at 400ºF for about 10-15 minutes. Continue to make more with remainder of apple salsa.

Serves 12

Calories 237; Fat 16g; Saturated Fat 6g; Carbohydrates 16g; Protein 6g; Sodium 192mg; Fiber 1g

chef tianna's tips:

This a great appetizer for the holidays. I recommend my favorite Honey Crisp Apples. Apple salsa is a great healthy snack for your children.

have an attitude
of gratitude

keeping it moving

We all have our struggles – regardless, we should give thanks. Let's not only give thanks for what we have, but also for what shall come to pass. There are so many things to be thankful for despite adversity, trials, tribulations and hard economic times. Choose an attitude of gratitude.

The year 2010, for me, was filled with many challenges, and peaks and valleys. I'm still taking the time to say thank you for family and friends. In 2010, my family and I were around the table together giving thanks for everything – our health, new beginnings, family reunions, and new jobs. My father is the person that I most remembered. Gathered around wonderful food, and great family and friends, my father stood proudly thanking God for that day. Although he's no longer with us, my father is definitely here in spirit. So, thank you, Daddy, for you, your life, and for your legacy. God bless you and may you rest in peace!

While enjoying meals, remember not to overindulge. Pace yourself! Think healthy first. Make sure you have a well-balanced plate with the following protein and vegetable options:

<u>Protein</u>
- Turkey
- Chicken
- Pork
- Fish

<u>Vegetables</u>
- Collard greens
- Kale
- Green beans
- Asparagus
- Spinach

Most importantly, eat complex carbohydrates, such as sweet potatoes. It is definitely healthy to have a lot of color on your plate. It is a joy to have days with family and friends to give thanks for the wonderful food that is indeed a blessing from God. Indulge your portions with moderation and balance. Please make sure that your body gets the healthy nutrients that it needs. And, no matter what your situations or circumstances, always be thankful.

keeping it moving

sautéed green beans w/ shallots

ingredients:

1 tbsp unsalted butter

2 tbsp sunflower oil

2 lb green beans, trimmed

Kosher salt and cracked black pepper

1 shallot peeled, and finely chopped

directions:

Before sautéing green beans blanch the green beans. Heat a 12 inch sauté pan over medium-high heat. Add the sunflower oil and butter, swirl to coat the pan. Then add your shallots and green beans. Sauté, stirring frequently, until the beans are bright green and crisp-tender, about 5-8 minutes. Season with salt and pepper to taste. Transfer the beans to a warmed serving bowl and garnish with the shallot crisps. Serve immediately. Have an Attitude of Gratitude, while eating this delicious dish.

Serves 4-6
Calories 148g; Fat 9g; Saturated Fat 2g; Carbohydrates 16.5g; Protein 4.25g; Sodium .25g; Fiber 7.75g

chef tianna's tips:

This is best served with brown rice or rice pilaf.

keeping it moving

make your own ("myo") grilled pizza

ingredients:

½ lb chicken sausage

1 tbsp of olive oil

1 red bell pepper, julienned or sliced

1 green bell pepper, julienned or sliced

½ large Vidalia onions

4 basil leaves

1 cup reduced fat Mozzarella cheese

4 tbsp marinara sauce

2 Tandoori naan flatbread

directions:

Remove casing from the sausage. Broil sausage at 425°F until golden brown and cooked through, about 10 minutes per side. Remove the sausage from the broiler and slice into ¼ inch thick slices.

Preheat grill to medium high heat. Brush one side of bread with olive oil and place on a sheet pan. Spread 2 tbsp of marinara on to one side of the bread. Top with peppers, onions, basil, cheese and sausage. Sprinkle with fresh ground pepper and carefully place on hot grill. Grill for a few minutes until bread has light grill marks and is slightly crisp. Close grill and let cook for about 4-5 minutes, checking for melting cheese. Once cheese is melted and bread is crisp, take off grill, slice and serve. Eat and enjoy while discussing with your children about *Have an Attitude of Gratitude*.

Serves 2-3

Calories 343; Fat 16g; Saturated Fat 8g; Carbohydrates 28g; Protein 21g; Sodium 871mg; Fiber 7g

chef tianna's tips:

This is a great way to make pizza in advance with your children and freeze for later. No more store-bought pizza. The thing about MYO pizza is that you can put whatever you like on your pizza, from chicken to different veggies. You name it, you can add it. Remember this is a great way to get that child who does not like vegetables to eat them. Serve this pizza along with a mixed green salad w/balsamic vinaigrette.

knowing what to
do and doing it

keeping it moving

When it comes to achieving a healthier eating lifestyle, there is often a big gap separating us from knowing and doing. What do you think it is? Is it procrastination? Fear? Not sure of the outcome? Lack of motivation? What can it be? Well, it can be all of these things. In life, there are many times when we know what to do but we choose not to do what we know. How can we take steps toward adopting a healthier eating lifestyle? How can we close the gap?

1. Identify where you are with your health. Ask yourself, "Currently, how are my eating and exercising habits?"
2. Identify things that you would like to change/incorporate in your daily routine.
3. Take small steps to improve your eating and exercising habits. Drink more water versus juice/soda and eat out less frequently. Also take short walks and increase the distance each time.

Knowing what to do and acting on it helps to control both internal and external risk factors that contribute to diseases and negative health conditions in the future.

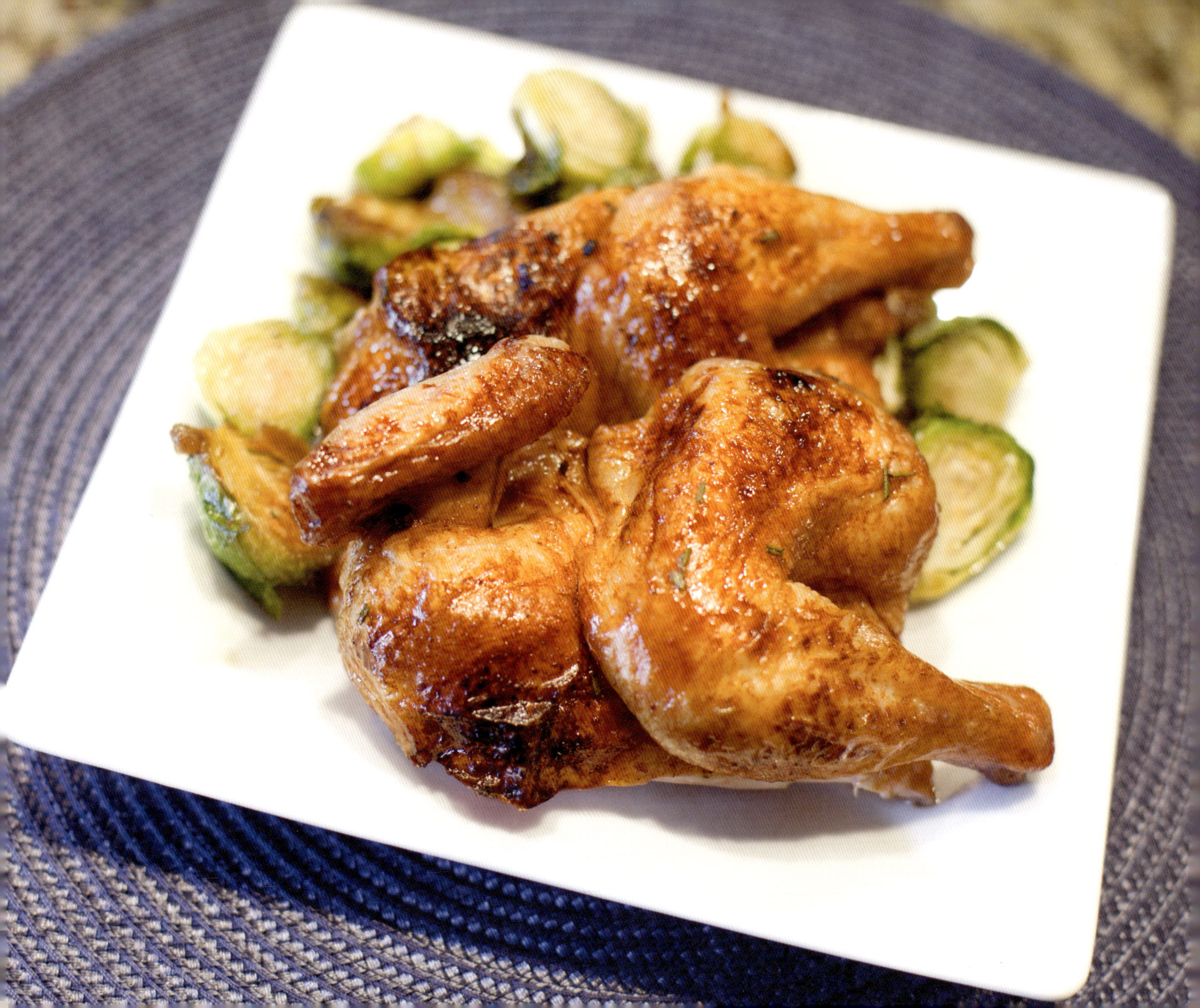

keeping it moving

roasted orange balsamic cornish hens

ingredients:

4 hens, rinse & pat dry

Kosher salt cracked black pepper

1 cup orange juice concentrate

1 cup balsamic vinegar

3 tbsp extra-virgin olive oil

5 stems fresh rosemary, chopped

directions:

Preheat oven to 425° F. Line two baking pans with foil. Split hens and butterfly. Open and place two hens on each baking pan. Season the hens with salt and pepper. Mix the orange concentrated juice, balsamic vinegar and olive oil and pour evenly over the hens. Sprinkle with rosemary and roast 15 minutes at 425° F and 30 minutes at 375°F. Place on plate and serve immediately. Eat and discuss *Knowing What to Do and Doing It (page 94)*.

Serves 8
Calories 343; Fat 16g; Saturated Fat 8g; Carbohydrates 28g; Protein 21g; Sodium 871mg; Fiber 7g

chef tianna's tips:

Here is an idea. Turn this into dinner by adding baked sweet potato and sautéed cabbage.

ch# the 4cs to a healthy lifestyle

keeping it moving

I was blessed with the opportunity, as a blogger, to participate in Steve Harvey's Disney's Dreamers Academy. I blogged about 100 students from across the nation who came to Disney World in Orlando, Florida. They attended to receive knowledge, wisdom and encouragement from inspirational keynote speakers, peers, business leaders, and celebrities. The speakers shared with the students about how they recognized and became passionate about their dreams. Throughout the weekend, Steve Harvey and the keynote speakers focused on the 4Cs that they believe start the journey toward fulfilling your dreams:

- Courage
- Confidence
- Consistency
- Curiosity

As I listened to the keynote speakers provide counsel about those 4Cs, I thought to myself that the same 4Cs can be applied to healthy lifestyle choices. Currently, one of my best friends is going through a weight loss program. I notice her confidence, courage, consistency and her curiosity. Actually, we can all have those characteristics. You have to decide and make CHOICES to follow through on positive commitments. If you can't follow through for yourself, you certainly can't follow through for anyone else. Here is how I believe we can apply the 4C's to having a healthy lifestyle.

1. Have CONFIDENCE within yourself to make changes. Remember, life is about choices. Make the right choices regarding your food selections, and exercise routines.
2. Be CONSISTENT. Continue to push yourself. Sometimes we make a lot of excuses. I understand it's hard but, we have the power within us to overcome those challenges.
3. Get CURIOUS about trying new foods. Step out of your comfort zone – again, are you comfortable with being comfortable?
4. Have COURAGE. Control your mindset, actions, and choices and believe that you can succeed. Don't be afraid to implement your new food and exercise changes. Don't bail out – dig in. Fear hinders and kills dreams. Faith motivates and leads to greatness. BE GREAT!

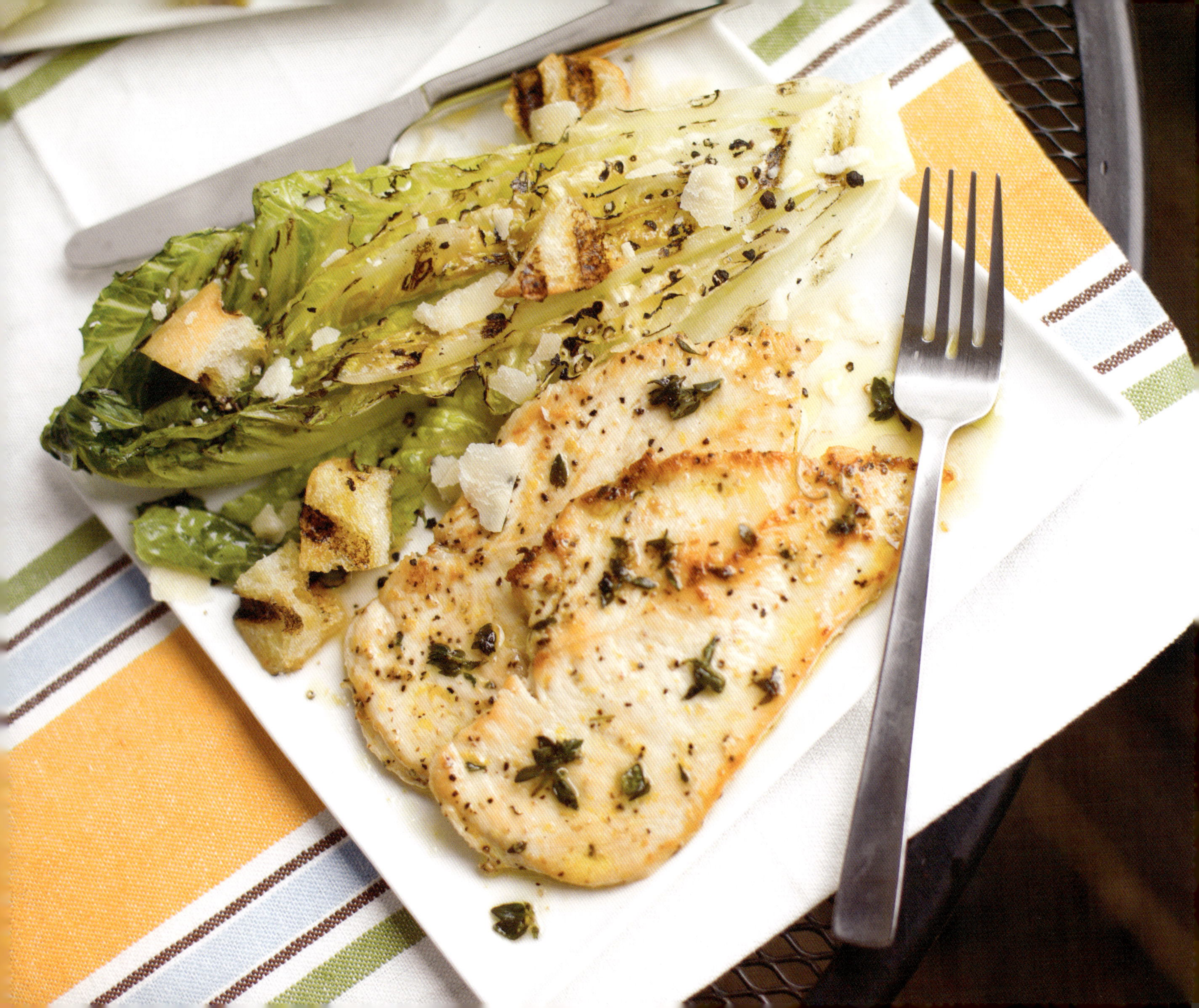

keeping it moving

grilled romaine lettuce w/ ciabatta bread (the croutons)

ingredients:

2 heads romaine lettuce

2 tbsp olive oil

½ cup fresh grated Parmesan cheese

Kosher salt & cracked black pepper

½ loaf ciabatta bread

directions:

Rinse and dry the head of romaine lettuce. Slice the romaine in two (length wise) pulling away a few leaves. Drizzle liberally with olive oil and add a little coarse salt and fresh cracked black pepper. Grate about a half cup of Parmesan cheese. Then grill the lettuce. Look for the lettuce to blacken a bit. The lettuce should have a nice char look to it without having it wilt too much under the heat. Sprinkle with cheese. Don't forget to take some time to read If There's a Will, There's a Way (page 64).

Cut ciabatta bread into 8 slices. Cut bread on a bias (diagonal). Drizzle bread with olive oil. Add salt and pepper. Grill bread slices over medium coals 2 minutes or until golden brown. Turn bread slices over, and grill an additional 2 minutes or until golden brown.

Serves 4
Calories 172; Fat 11.5g; Saturated Fat 3.5g; Carbohydrates 11g; Protein 9.25g; Sodium 411mg; Fiber 6.75g

chef tianna's tips:

If you are going to be grilling chicken breasts, you can always slice the chicken breast and serve with your grilled Romaine lettuce.

pay now or
pay later

keeping it moving

I've learned that being a personal chef is more than just preparing food for people – it is about expressing love, and bringing people together through food. In addition to providing healthy dishes, I have a passion for helping others to improve their lifestyles. My approach is holistic, which includes balancing overall good health in mind, body, and soul. As a woman who had fibroids, I have watched our African American community suffer with heart disease and high cholesterol. This has caused me to be extremely health conscious.

When it comes to grocery shopping and selecting healthy foods, we tend to go with less expensive options. I've had many people tell me "Oh, eating healthy is too expensive." My response is "so is chemo." You need to ask yourself "Do I pay now or pay later?" Everything we do in life is an investment. It is best to pay for healthy food choices now versus paying high healthcare costs–due to illness later. I know that we need to stretch our finances, so there is a way to ease the sting regarding money matters – shop seasonally, and give earnest attention to products that are "on sale." Shopping seasonally usually means the seasonal foods are available at lower prices than foods that aren't in season. Consider apples; they have many uses. Not only are apples healthy, tasty and high in fiber, they can also be INEXPENSIVE. Apples have 5 grams of fiber and are 85 percent water. We do need our fiber for healthy digestion. Apples help lower cholesterol, reduce cancer risks, and assist with weight loss. When on the go, apples are a quick snack to give kids. My favorite apple is the Honey Crisp. It tastes like honey and actually makes a crispy sound - delish! Apples can be used in all types of dishes, such as chicken and garden salads or stewed for a side dish.

keeping it moving

harvest salad w/turkey tenderloins

ingredients:

1 lb turkey tenderloins

2 tbsp olive oil

Salt and pepper

Vinaigrette

¼ cup red wine vinegar

¼ cup fresh lemon juice

1 tsp honey

2 tbsp fresh basil, minced

1 cup olive oil

Salad

1 lb mixed greens

2 cups honey crisp apples

½ cup red seedless grapes, halved

½ cup dried cranberries

½ cup diced dates

½ cup pecans, toasted

directions:

Rub the turkey tenderloins with oil, then salt and pepper. Cook the tenderloins on medium-high in skillet until browned. Remove and set aside. To prepare the vinaigrette, whisk together red vinegar, lemon juice, honey, and minced basil. In a thin stream, whisk in the olive oil until well incorporated. Set aside. Slice the turkey into thin strips. Toss together mixed greens, apples, seedless grapes, dried cranberries, diced dates, and toasted pecans. Place the turkey on top. Drizzle with the dressing. While enjoying this healthy dish, read Pay Now or Pay Later (page 102).

Serves 4

Calories 360; Fat 19g; Saturated Fat 2g; Carbohydrates 31g; Protein 19g; Sodium 178mg; Fiber 1.2g

chef tianna's tips:

Honey Crisp is my favorite apple with this dish however; it is a seasonal fruit in some places. Feel free to use any apple EXCEPT Red Delicious!!!

keeping it moving

champagne mango & basil salsa

ingredients:

2 large, ripe champagne mango, peeled, pitted and diced (about 1 ½ cups)

¾ cup red onion, finely chopped

6 large fresh basil leaves, chopped

Juice of one fresh lime

2 tbsp apple cider vinegar

Sea salt & pepper to taste

directions:

Combine all of the ingredients in a bowl. Season to taste with salt and pepper. Eat and enjoy!

Serves 3
Calories 129; Fat: .5g; Saturated Fat 0; Carbohydrates 32g; Protein 2g; Sodium 311mg; Fiber 3.5g

chef tianna's tips:

Great snack with baked tortilla chips. Also great when served with jerk chicken or as a great condiment for a burger.

cool things to know about food and you

Juvonia Harris RD, LDN, Maryland

Apples-Honey Crisp: One medium honey crisp apple has 5 grams of fiber and only 80 calories. Because of the amount and type of fiber, an apple will help a person feel full longer, helping him or her to consume fewer calories daily. The pectin in apples may also help lower cholesterol. The flesh and peel are packed with disease-fighting antioxidants and phytochemicals that may protect against breast and lung cancer. These-fighting nutrients work best when the peel and flesh are eaten together.

Arugula: Good source of vitamin A and C; provides energy; improves blood quality.

Asparagus: It contains vitamin A, C and E.

Basil: Good source of vitamin A, which helps to prevent damage to the cells by free radicals. Vitamin A also prevents free radical from oxidizing cholesterol in the blood stream, preventing the cholesterol from building up in the blood vessels.

Brussel Sprouts: Loaded with vitamin A, folacin, potassium, and calcium. This has 3-5 grams of fiber per cup.

Butternut Squash: A well-balanced food source that is rich in complex carbohydrates and low in saturated fat and sodium. It is a very good source of vitamins A and C and a good source of beta-carotene, magnesium, manganese, calcium, and potassium.

Cabbage: Abundant in vitamin C; richer in vitamin C than orange juice. Cabbage is a low-glycemic food, which will help control blood sugar and insulin.

Celery: High in dietary fiber, high in vitamins A, B2, B5, B6, C and K; high in minerals, calcium, magnesium, phosphorus, and potassium; low in saturated fat and cholesterol.

Cilantro: An herb that contains no cholesterol; but is rich in antioxidants and dietary fiber which help reduce LDL or "bad cholesterol" while increasing HDL or "good cholesterol" levels.

Cranberry: Because they contain flavonoids, studies reported by WebMD Medial News suggest cranberry can be a weapon in the war against atherosclerosis. Flavonoids help reduce the amount of bad cholesterol in your system.

Dates: This is termed to be a laxative food. Dates are beneficial for people suffering from constipation and can help those struggling with regularity. For getting the best laxative effect from dates, you need to soak dates for one night in water until plump.

Egg Whites: Contains no cholesterol.

Garlic: Modern science has shown that garlic is a powerful natural antibiotic.

Green Beans: Excellent source of vitamin K, fiber, C and A. Also helps with maintaining strong bones.

Kale: Great source of vitamins A, C and K; great antioxidant and promotes healthy skin. Kale is loaded with fiber which can help to lower cholesterol. Wonderful source of calcium also!

Lemons: Lemon juice mixed with lukewarm water and honey can reduce body weight. Lemons help to flush bacteria and toxins from the body.

Limes: Great source of vitamin C. Lime juice is said to be good for the skin.

Olive Oil: Olive oil has many, many benefits. It contains antioxidants and is a monounsaturated "good" fat. One tablespoon of this oil can help relieve constipation.

Onions: A part of the Allium family and provide health benefits when eaten, much like garlic. Onions can help to prevent bacterial infection.
Parsley: A regular garnish of parsley can help ward off cardiovascular disease, such as heart attack, stroke, and atherosclerosis. It's more than just a garnish. Parsley can be boiled to make a yummy tea that helps remove excess fluid.
Red Potatoes: Fat-free, cholesterol-free, very low sodium and a good source of fiber. Red potatoes also contain vitamin C.
Romaine Lettuce: Rich in potassium, which helps in bringing down high blood pressure, another cause of heart disease.
Rosemary: People can chew the leaves of the rosemary plant or make a tea from the leaves in order to soothe the stomach or relieve symptoms from irritable bowel syndrome.
Sage: It flourishes the body with iron, by boosting the iron stores in the body, hence, increases energy.
• It has recently been proven that taking sage can improve and enhance one's memory.
• Sage is very good source of vitamin A, calcium, iron and potassium. Vitamin A and calcium and are both especially important for maintaining healthy teeth, bones and skin.
Salmon: Also known as a superfood. Salmon is loaded with Omega-3 fatty acids and can improve heart health as well as support proper brain function.
Shallots: Have more antioxidants, minerals, and vitamins on weight per weight basis than onions.
Shrimp: The iodine in shrimp is good for the proper functioning of the thyroid gland which controls the basal metabolic rate. Iodine deficiency can result in sluggish thyroid activity which can lead to weight gain or hinder weight loss.
Strawberries: Strawberries contain more vitamin C than an orange. They are rich in folate, potassium and are a good source of fiber.
Sweet Potatoes: Rich in beta-carotene and meets your daily need for vitamin A. It also provides nearly a third of vitamin C that is recommend each day. Sweet Potatoes contain vitamin C, potassium and fiber.
Swiss Chard: Good source of fiber. Rich source of omega -3 fatty acids. It is very rich in vitamin A, C and K.
Thyme: The thyme extract thymol is one of the ingredients in the antibacterial Listerine mouthwash. Thyme also contains a variety of flavonoids and is a good source of iron and manganese.
Tomatoes: Contains lycopene (the red pigment in tomato). Tomatoes are powerful antioxidants. Pair with broccoli for immune building benefits.
Turkey Bacon: Lower in fat and calories than pork bacon.
Turnips: Rich in vitamin C; prevents inflammation; builds blood; great immune system support.
Vinegar -Apple Cider: Powerful cleansing and healing elixir. Apple cider vinegar contains a naturally occurring antibiotic and antiseptic that fights germs and bacteria. Choose an Apple Cider Vinegar that is dark and "cloudy" at the bottom which is usually organic.
White Potatoes: One large potato is a great source of vitamin C. Potatoes are also a great source of multiple B vitamins which support the nervous system.
Yogurt: Yogurt is a good source of calcium and protein. It is a probiotic because of the live cultures of lactobacillus acidophilus. Yogurt can help to replenish the "good" bacteria that your body needs.

recipe index

early bird smoothie	5
broiled chicken salad w/tarragon & cranberries	8
roasted asparagus	9
fish tacos w/spicy chipotle remoulade	13
sautéed rainbow swiss chard	19
turkey bacon & veggie frittata	23
turkey chili	26
seared scallops w/pepper & tarragon sauce	27
grilled tuscan skirt steak	33
lemon thyme herbed chicken marinade	36
phillip's turnips	37
low fat mac & cheese w/ shrimp	40
sautéed kale	41
egg scrambler	44
pecan crusted chicken	45
butternut squash orzo w/sage	49
whole wheat linguine w/shrimp, tomatoes basil	53
roasted brussel sprouts	58
twice baked sweet potatoes	59
roasted sweet & white potatoes w/shallots & sage	63
the real deal phil burger	67
breakfast wrap	70
watermelon w/arugula & mint vinaigrette	71
brunch quiche	75
lemon herbed tilapia	79
chicken stew	85
crunchy cornflake chicken tenders	88
apple salsa & brie puff pastry	89
sautéed green beans	92
make your own (myo) grilled pizza	93
roasted orange balsamic cornish hens	97
grilled romaine lettuce w/ciabatta bread	101
harvest salad w/turkey tenderloins	104
champagne mango & basil salsa	105